Wild LAKE MICHIGAN

John and Ann Mahan

Foreword by
Jerry Sullivan and Glenda Daniel

VOYAGEUR PRESS

To our parents, who fostered our love of the natural world, and to our daughters Jennifer and Kristen, who share our adventures and enrich our lives.

Printed in Hong Kong through Bookbuilders Ltd.
91 92 93 94 95 5 4 3 2 1

Library of Congress Cataloging-in-Publication Data

Mahan, John.
    Wild Lake Michigan / by John & Ann Mahan.
        p. cm.
    Includes bibliographical references and index.
    ISBN 0-89658-132-2
    1. Natural history — Michigan, Lake. 2. Lake ecology — Michigan,
Lake. 3. Michigan, Lake. I. Mahan, Ann. II. Title.
QH104.5.M44M35 1991
508.774 — dc20   90-24427
                                                      CIP

Published by
Voyageur Press, Inc.
P.O. Box 338
123 North Second Street
Stillwater, MN 55082 U.S.A.
In Minn 612-430-2210
Toll-free 800-888-9653

Voyageur Press books are also available at discounts for quantities for educational, fundraising, premium, or sales-promotion use. For details contact the marketing department. Please write or call for our free catalog of natural history publications.

CONTENTS

ACKNOWLEDGMENTS

Speak to the earth, and it shall teach thee.

Job 12:8 (King James Version)

Special thanks to the following people who reviewed chapters regarding their fields of expertise and made suggestions: Bob Birmingham (archaeology), Terri Bussey (Native Americans), Glenda Daniel and Jerry Sullivan (North Woods and wetlands), Jim Ludwig (lake ecology), Ken Potts (maritime history), Lloyd Schmaltz (geology), and Earl Wolf (dunes).

We also are grateful to those who graciously shared their knowledge: David Devault (E.P.A.), Marg Dochoda (Great Lakes Fishery Commission), Joan Freeman (Wisconsin State Archaeologist), John Halsey (Michigan State Archaeologist), H. J. Harris (University of Wisconsin, Sea Grant Institute), Donald Heldman (archaeologist, Michilimackinac State Park), Harold Humphrey (epidemiologist, Michigan Department of Health), Jim Kitchell (University of Wisconsin Limnology Lab), Ann Lindsay (Center for the Great Lakes), Harry Lippincott (National Ocean Service), Frank Quinn (chief hydrologist, Great Lakes Environmental Research Laboratory), William Scharf (biologist, Northwestern Michigan College), and Asa Wright (Michigan D.N.R.).

Thanks to the librarians of the Lincoln Township Library in Stevensville, Michigan, for their friendship and assistance through the many hours we spent in their company. In our Lake Michigan travels, we have appreciated the many helpful park rangers and nature center naturalists, and especially our fellow campers, who shared their insights with us.

FOREWORD

This is a book that can help us learn how to think about the natural world. As a culture, our style has been to divide things, to think of humanity as totally separate from nature, and to further split nature into geology, zoology, botany, meteorology, and a host of ever finer subdivisions. This approach has given us a great deal of knowledge about the way the world works, but it does tend to disguise *the* fundamental truth about our planet: Everything here is connected to everything else. This connectedness is not some mock-profundity for poetic souls to muse on while they watch the sun setting over Lake Michigan; it is the hardest of cold, hard facts.

John and Ann Mahan have artfully combined research and experience to give us a book that places human history in the natural context of Lake Michigan. They tell all the stories we know about the lake, including the stories of Native Americans and the stories of geologists. They tell us the ways we have harmed the lake and how we can undo that harm. They show us a way to perceive the lake that starts with the realization of the connectedness of all things.

JERRY SULLIVAN AND GLENDA DANIEL

Jerry Sullivan and Glenda Daniel are co-authors of *A Sierra Club Naturalist's Guide to the North Woods*. Glenda Daniel is also Executive Director of Lake Michigan Federation, and author of *Dune Country*, an ecological guide to the Indiana Dunes.

LAKE SUPERIOR

LAKE MICHIGAN
BASIN

MICHIGAN

Naubinway

STONINGTON
PENINSULA

BEAVER
ISLANDS

ST. HELENA
ISLAND
Straits of Mackinac

St. Ignace

LAKE
HURON

Escanaba

GARDEN
PENINSULA

ILE AUX
GALETS

WILDERNESS
STATE PARK

WISCONSIN

ROCK ISLAND

FOX
ISLANDS

LAKE MICHIGAN
BASIN

Porte des Morts

WASHINGTON ISLAND

LEELANAU
PENINSULA

Grand
Traverse
Bay

PENINSULA
STATE PARK

NEWPORT
STATE PARK

MANITOU
ISLANDS

OLD MISSION
PENINSULA

DOOR
PENINSULA

CANA ISLAND

RIDGES
SANCTUARY

Green Bay

CAVE POINT

Platte Bay Empire

Skegemog Swamp

NORTH WOODS

Traverse City

SLEEPING BEAR
DUNES

Green Bay

NORTH WOODS

Kewaunee

POINT BEACH
STATE FOREST *

NORDHOUSE DUNES

Manitowoc

LUDINGTON
STATE PARK   Ludington

TENSION ZONE

Sheboygan

KETTLE MORAINE

KOHLER–ANDRAE
STATE PARK

SILVER LAKE
STATE PARK

TENSION ZONE

MICHIGAN

LIZARD MOUND PARK

HARRINGTON BEACH
STATE PARK

MUSKEGON
STATE PARK

P.J. HOFFMASTER
STATE PARK

LAKE MICHIGAN

GRAND HAVEN
STATE PARK

LAKE MICHIGAN
BASIN

Milwaukee

WISCONSIN

HOLLAND
STATE PARK

SAUGATUCK DUNES
STATE PARK

CHIWAUKEE
PRAIRIE
*

ILLINOIS BEACH
STATE PARK *

VAN BUREN
STATE PARK

St. Joseph

NORTH WOODS

TENSION ZONE

Chicago

GRAND MERE
STATE PARK

WARREN DUNES
STATE PARK

ILLINOIS

Gary

INDIANA
DUNES

South Bend

LAKE MICHIGAN
BASIN

INDIANA

LAND AND WATER

DUNES

For countless years the waves have thundered upon the beach and the ripples have murmured along it. Their music is recorded in the sands.
— *J. Ronald Engel*

To walk in the dunes is to walk through time. These miniscule grains of quartz that gather together to make such a magnificent community were created long before the coming of humans. Children of the glaciers and wards of the wind, they have for millennia washed and drifted, bounced and tumbled from one age to the next.

These sands are an end product of a long line of events. For over one million years, massive glaciers of the Pleistocene Ice Age advanced and retreated across the northern half of the North American continent, grinding and pulverizing rock, while transporting the debris in their icy travels. With the final glacial retreat some 10,000 years ago, the long process of distribution was taken over by rivers, lake currents, and wind. Sandbars created 4,000 years ago by the higher water levels of Lake Michigan's ancestor, Lake Nipissing, became vast sand beaches when water levels receded. With the sculpting of these exposed beaches by westerly winds, Lake Michigan's dunes were born.

Ancient sands continue to wash and drift into dunes along modern Lake Michigan. And long after we are gone, the sand will still be here, or there, or somewhere, ever shifting and drifting. These sands of time have a profound effect on visitors, connecting them with the timelessness of the elements and the natural processes.

Paradoxically, in spite of their antiquity, the sands collectively are an example of geology in fast forward. Dunes are never the same from one day to the next. Indeed, in a strong wind the transformation takes place before our very eyes.

Walking from beach to foredune, and beyond, we observe plant succession and progression since Lake Nipissing. Entire worlds exist with their citizens going about their lives in spaces no larger than a city backyard, sometimes smaller. These dune dwellers live in close proximity, just across the ecological transition line from nearby neighbors that are, nonetheless, worlds apart.

The wave-swept shoreline beach is a harsh environment virtually devoid of plant life. Here sand and gravel are moved and sorted, washed and smoothed. During times of high wind and waves, the beach is torn and tossed about; during times of low wind and gentle waves, it is caressed and smoothed over. Messengers of the sweetwater sea, the waves are in constant communication with the beach—sometimes whispering, sometimes roaring. And, as in all transactions, something is gained and something lost. Sand is picked up here and put down there. The bleached bones of wrecked sailing vessels from another time are covered and uncovered, washed in and pulled out.

This is a place of trash and treasures, the definition of which is entirely in the eye, or stomach, of the beholder. Sandpipers, plovers, and sanderlings dart back and forth before the wave edges, snatching insects and crustaceans. In much the same manner, a child moves back and forth, hoping the multicolored and polished pebble washed away by the last wave will return with the next. And just down the beach, herring gulls scrabble and shout at each other over the carcass of a beached chinook salmon. Oblivious to all this, a couple lost in its reverie walks on the singing sands—the wet beach

Wind-sculpted sand at Sleeping Bear Dunes.

Lake Michigan's shoreline.

A sandpiper combs the shoreline for edible treasures at Point Beach State Forest.

along the water's edge, where friction of footsteps on moist quartz grains produces a faint, high-pitched tone.

Plant life, so conspicuously absent on the active lower beach, begins to take hold in the middle beach. This is an area of temporary summer refuge for a few hardy residents such as sea rocket, bugseed, and seaside spurge. Although but a few feet from a vast water supply, the surface of the midbeach has more in common with the desert—hot, dry, and windy. The few plants courageous enough to brave this environment are all business, with no need or tolerance of beauty and extravagance.

Sea rocket holds water in its succulent tissues, fighting water loss with its smooth and glossy leaves. Seaside spurge takes itself out of the wind by branching out and hugging the sand, at the same time avoiding excess water loss by growing small, narrow leaves. Bugseed also fights water loss with small, narrow leaves. All three plants conserve resources by producing small, nondescript flowers and equally small and economical seeds. With their work done and seeds set, they close up shop and die—just in time for autumn storms to push waves higher up the beach, washing

plants of the midbeach from their moorings, rolling and tumbling them and depositing their seeds up and down the shore.

The midbeach is also an area of increasing animal life: tiger beetles, burrowing spiders, and adventurous ants. During the fall mating season, ladybird beetles mass on driftwood by the thousands.

Permanent residence isn't found in the midbeach. Only on the upper beach and beyond, out of reach of all but the most violent storm waves, do plants set up long-term housekeeping. This upper beach is also where dune building begins with the stars of dune creation: marram grass (beach grass) and cottonwood seedlings. Here is the birthplace of the foredunes, the latest in a series of sand waves marching inland, increasingly slowed down by the resistance of successively larger plant loads.

All plants contribute to dune building by slowing wind and creating eddies where windblown sand is deposited, causing even greater wind resistance and sand deposition. Cottonwoods and marram grass are champions in this process due to their rare ability to survive sand burial. The marram grass plant spreads by rhizome propagation, sending down and out an un-

Unstable dunes at Lincoln Township Nature Center, near Grand Mere State Park.

derground stem that sprouts roots and sends up new plants. One plant may eventually spread twenty feet or more. As the dune grows in depth (up to ten feet), the central stem keeps its leaves in sunlight by internodal elongation. The length of the segment between each stem joint, called an internode, is determined by the rate and depth of dune growth. When dune growth slows sufficiently, creation of internodes still continues, pushing the stem above the dune's surface, eventually killing the plant. At this point the dune has been sufficiently stabilized, the job of marram grass is done, and the first stage of plant succession in the dunes is completed. With sand burial sufficiently checked, sand reed, little bluestem grass, and sand cherry bushes set up housekeeping, along with juniper, prickly pear cactus, evening primrose, hairy puccoon, pitcher's thistle, and a whole parade of their compatriots.

To walk into the older dunes is to walk through a living history of plant succession, as one plant type after another springs up — dependent on the stabilizing and nutrient building of the pioneering plants that went before it. Each plant community in turn creates a new environment more conducive to the succession of plants to follow.

The first tree to arrive is the cottonwood, the only tree capable of surviving the severe climate and sand burial of the foredunes. This is a tree of unique capabilities. As the dune builds higher and higher around a cottonwood's trunk, the tree responds by sending out new roots from the buried trunk while the rapidly growing top keeps its leaves above the rising dune surface. In dune country it is a common, but nonetheless startling, experience to stand next to a grove of small cottonwoods and realize they may be tops of hundred-year-old mature trees with over fifty feet of trunks buried below the dune!

Jack pine is usually one of the next trees to colonize the dunes, followed by red pine and oak, aspen, white pine, and finally maple, beech, and hemlock. Each successive tree species requires more nutrients, more seed germination and growth time — all dependent on the stabilizing and enriching work of their predecessors. Each successive tree has a typical understory growth that accompanies it. All of these successions work toward a climax environment, the mixed hardwood dune.

Farthest inland, this mixed hardwood dune looks remarkably undunelike. A mixture of oak, maple, and

Sand reed grass, marram grass, and cottonwoods stabilize a foredune at Grand Mere State Park.

Prickly pear cactus blossoms at Indiana Dunes National Lakeshore.

The back side of a blowout engulfs a previously stabilized hardwood dune.

14

A dune blowout at sunset.

beech, along with hemlock, white pine, and cedar, dominates a variable mix of understory trees. This is an area of distinctly deep woods flavor, with a high and cathedral-like canopy. Hardwood dune inhabitants, such as red fox and whitetail deer, are those typical of other mixed hardwood forests. The forest floor heralds spring with the delicate flowers of hepatica and fragrant trailing arbutus, followed by trilliums and, in some areas, morel mushrooms. In summer, the appearance is much like any North Woods mixed hardwood forest—deep, green, peaceful.

But make no mistake, this is still a dune underneath. Just a few bites of the shovel bring up pure sand. The hardwood dune still has the same capricious nature as its younger and more restless siblings. One set of ruts cut by off-road vehicle operators can reverse hundreds, even thousands, of years of dune building and plant succession as exposed sand careens off with the wind. Roots are bared to the elements, causing trees to die and fall victim to the wind; roots of toppling trees pull up thin surface soil, exposing even more sand to the wind's power and whimsy. As this process continues, a large horseshoe-shaped excavation is created, its open end pointing windward.

These natural amphitheaters are commonly called blowouts. They are a prominent feature of the dune landscape, occurring from natural, as well as human, disturbances. As the blowout deepens, excavated sand rolls over the top—progressively burying, killing, and then re-excavating trees, leaving the bleached bones of a ghost forest.

The sands shift and drift; the blowout becomes deeper and larger. Eventually it becomes so large that the effects of the wind are lessened and new dunes are formed to windward. At this point dune building and stabilization begin again, as the first cottonwood sprouts in the blowout's damp central depression and marram grass advances along the edges.

Life in the dunes is hard, sharp-edged, and real. Sand stings the face, bringing a pleasantly painful reality—there is no buffering from life here, no numbing of the senses from false overstimulation. There is no tolerance for pretense and wasted energy; what is important and real is evident, what isn't is quite literally blown away.

The dunes are a place of great struggle, of individual and community interdependence. The metaphors and analogies blowing through these rolling wilds are too insistent to be ignored. Just as members of the foredune communities make life possible for the downwind communities, so do we humans

Sand movement continues even in winter among the near-shore dunes.

need each other — and all of creation.

Wandering across the dunes, we see the interdependence of these sandy communities with the watery world that borders and so strongly influences the dunes. At the water's edge our bare feet, overheated from strolling the beach, suddenly feel the contrast of two adjacent environments as cool waves engulf them. In only a few steps we have walked from near desert to inland sea.

Wading in Lake Michigan's rolling surf, we marvel at the magnitude and beauty of the sweeping expanse of water before us. Here in the heart of the North American continent lies an inland freshwater sea that remains a watery wilderness — 22,300 square miles of an uninhabited, untamed fluid environment. Lake Michigan and her four sister Great Lakes are unique in all the world, containing 20 percent of the world's fresh water, and remaining the largest and most lasting evidence of the comings and goings of great glaciers.

The dunes are an indirect gift of the glaciers. While these mountains of sand appear along other Great Lakes, the dunes that drift along Lake Michigan's eastern and southern shores form the largest expanse of freshwater dunes in the world. Here we see the connectedness of land, wind, and sea, and of both large and small ecosystems.

Lake Michigan beach and forested dunes at Empire Bluffs.

THE
LAKE

I walked down to the water's edge tonight, lured by the luminous pull of the full moon. Sitting on that serenely bright beach, devoid of any other human presence, I watched as each wave crest picked up its bundle of pale light and carried it shimmering and bouncing until it spread its celestial gift gently at my feet. And all the while the waves' never-ending mantra whispered its way into my soul, bringing light and hope and a communion with the presence of all things.
—John's diary, September 16, 1989

Lake Michigan exerts an irresistible pull. What's out there? What's in there? It has faraway places, unseen distant shores, and shimmering islands floating on the horizon. Humans flock to the water's edge and look into its vastness; sooner or later, nearly all of us lean down and touch the water. This simple ritual brings us closer to the lake's wild essence.

But what is out there? And in there? Much more and considerably less than we ever imagined. More in terms of its abilities to provide for our needs, both physical and emotional. Less in terms of its abilities to absorb our abuses and mistakes.

Stretching just over 300 miles north to south and 118 miles east to west, Lake Michigan passes through nearly 5 degrees of latitude and 3 degrees of longitude—connecting two time zones and nearly thirteen millennia of human history. The lake's shorelines extend over 1,600 miles, encompassing four states: Indiana and Illinois to the south, Wisconsin to the west, and Michigan to the east and north. Lake Michigan is the largest body of fresh water lying entirely within the United States, the second largest of the Great Lakes (in volume), and the fifth largest freshwater lake in the world.

This is a lake of contrasts, from the industrial and nearly used up southwestern shores to the wild and relatively undeveloped northern shores. Sheer limestone cliffs tower along the shores of Door County and the Garden Peninsula, while to the east and south the shores are rimmed with soft mountainous dunes of windblown sand. Prickly pear cactuses bloom on the Indiana Dunes, convinced that they are residing in the desert, while boreal components of the North Woods march assertively down to the water's edge along areas of the north shore. In between, the mixed hardwood component of the North Woods merges with rolling dunes to the east and prairie remnants to the west.

Smooth in contour and with open horizons over much of its length, Lake Michigan changes abruptly in its northern third, sprouting five peninsulas and more than sixty named islands. Underwater, Lake Michigan is separated into north and south basins by a ridge of Silurian dolimitic limestone running from Muskegon to Milwaukee. The southern basin is the shallower of the two, while the north basin plunges to depths of nearly 1,000 feet.

Lake Michigan is a paradox conceived in rocks and born of ice. It is, geologically, an infant cradled in an ancient foundation. Geographically too large to appear fragile and too small to be given its due, it is to this day misunderstood, mislabeled, and misused. But in spite of our abuses, in spite of our misconceptions, it is still a wild and sweet sea. This magnificent ever-changing lake, with its surrounding dunes, forests, and wetlands, is a testament to the permanence of change. It refuses to be taken for granted. Just when we feel

Lake Michigan.

18

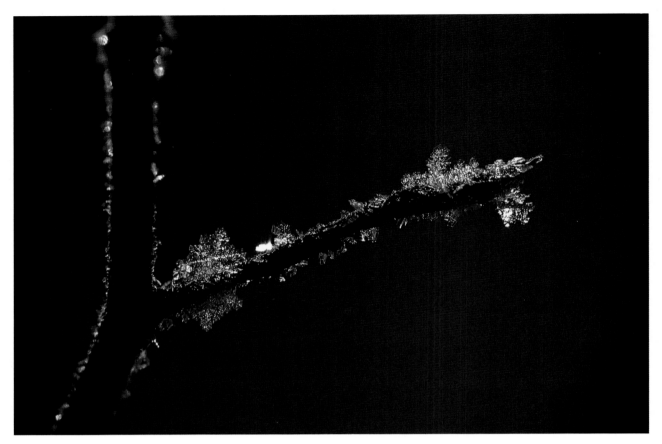

Hoarfrost crystals, Newport State Park.

The car ferry Badger *emerges from Lake Michigan's fog as it nears the Kewaunee Pierhead Light.*

comfortable and complacent, the water moves and rises — eroding and swallowing homes and businesses. And just as rapidly, its level drops, forcing us to switch from seawall building to channel dredging.

Lake Michigan is alive with wildness. True, it is a lake wounded and scarred by human attempts to tame and use it. But for many of us, its wildness is still its most immediate and compelling characteristic — a characteristic that must be seen and experienced to comprehend. Here are mysteries yet unraveled, wildness still untamed, and inland seas still alive with surprise.

LAKE EFFECT

Just as the lake has a profound effect on the human souls that gravitate to its shores and waters, so it defines and molds the islands and shoreline it embraces for many miles inland. It plays a starring role in determining what plants and animals reside here, and what human activities take place. However, the most immediate and obvious result of "lake effect" is the moderating, modifying, and sometimes intensifying of weather systems brought about by the thermal storage capacity of Lake Michigan's 1,180 cubic miles of water.

This massive solar heat collector exerts a mild and friendly effect on temperatures for several miles inland, resulting in cooler summers and milder winters. With prevailing westerly winds, the eastern shoreline, as well as the Door, Leelanau, and Old Mission peninsulas, are primary recipients of the lake's moderating effects on temperature. Fruiting plants have found this extended frost-free season and the warm moist lake breezes to their liking. In his diary of 1679, Father Louis Hennepin described wild "ripe grapes, large as damson plums," which he and French explorer La Salle's men made into wine, and ate with bearmeat at the site of present-day St. Joseph, Michigan.

While moderating temperatures, the lake also functions as an immense humidifier, intermittently creating stifling summer humidity at the southern end, frequent fogs, delicate hoarfrost, and the infamous lake effect snows of the lee shores.

Three basic types of fog are experienced around and over the lake. Advection fog forms where warm air flows over cooler water. This fog is common in spring and early summer around the shores as well as over the open waters — the densest and most persistent fog. It is the fog that makes sailors place radar reflectors in their rigging before entering the busy shipping lanes, such as the Manitou Passage — or wish they had, while listening to the low rumble of freighters' engines and the eerie echoing of foghorns drifting in and out of the ether without any apparent direction. This is the fog that is so persistent over the northwest portions of the lake when cooler upwelling water replaces surface water blown across the lake by westerly winds.

On cool, clear fall nights, radiation fog is created as land loses heat to the air, causing a warm air layer over a low-lying cold air mass that condenses moisture. Forming onshore in valleys and lowlands, these ground clouds often drift over the lake in the early morning, burning off by noon.

Steam fog, known also as arctic sea smoke, is a thin, smoky, ethereal fog that wisps and dances over the lake on cold winter nights and mornings. Less frequently seen, this fog of delicate beauty may combine with shoreline features to create even more exquisite and fleeting works of art — hoarfrost.

We experienced this phenomenon while winter camping at Newport State Park, near the tip of the Door Peninsula. Weather conditions had been disappointing, with leaden featureless skies and the gray day atmosphere of a low-pressure system — not the kind of day two camera-laden, winter-camping, very hopeful photographers had counted on. Once again, we were reminded that the natural world has its own agenda.

Later in the day a cold front began to push in with characteristic intensity, resulting in near blizzard conditions — a day many people would spend indoors, grumbling at mounting snowdrifts through fogged-up windows. For us, blizzards are one of the most exhilarating times to be outside; and we spent the rest of the day skiing through the wild vigor and rare solitude of that storm. As the storm was blowing itself out, we returned to camp, and a tent that had nearly been swept away. Wind had excavated the tent pegs bare; only the excess weight in our packs, which we had cursed on the trail, had kept the tent from becoming airborne.

Later that evening, as the high-pressure system asserted itself, the temperature plummeted and the sky became piercingly clear. Stars shone with an uncommon brightness seen only on such remote winter evenings far from the glare of city lights. In that wonderful crisp wintry night, conditions were excellent for the formation of hoarfrost: a source of water vapor (the warm lake), the temperature dropping below freezing (a winter high-pressure air mass), and something very cold on which to crystallize (our small shoreline point with winter-bare limbs and twigs).

The next morning, steam fog wisped and danced over the open lake. Every twig and branch was covered with the fairy-world fans and needles of hoarfrost crystals. Nature had provided two very hopeful photographers with more than they came seeking: an exhilarating blizzard to ski through, hoarfrost crystals to photograph, and this story to share.

During winter months, prevailing winds shift more northwesterly, bringing polar air masses to the region. As these cold, dry winds blow across the lake, they pick up warmth and moisture from the open waters. Cooled again as it approaches land, this moisture precipitates into heavy snows, turning virtually the entire easterly shore into one long snowbelt. In the northern third of Michigan's lower peninsula, snowbelt conditions extend more than halfway across the state, making this area one of the Upper Midwest's prime winter playgrounds. Lake-effect snows have a capricious nature, depending on wind direction. Fingers of snowfall reach inland from the lake, covering various locations in a heavy blanket of snow, while only dusting neighboring communities with flurries. Traveling along the Lake Michigan coastline, you may drive through alternating bright sun and blinding blizzards.

While the lake often has a moderating effect on weather, the weather doesn't always reciprocate. With regard to erosion, the weather's effect on the lake is anything but moderate. Lakeshore erosion is primarily a phenomenon of the fall, early winter, and spring seasons—these are the seasons of strong winds and high seas, the main cause of shoreline erosion. By midwinter, ice floes have been distributed by wind and currents along the lakeshore, forming attached windrows that inhibit shoreline erosion. Ice may extend ten to twenty miles into the lake, with an average surface coverage of 40 percent (80 percent in severe winters, 10 percent in mild winters).

The ice that is protective in midwinter undergoes a Jekyll-and-Hyde role reversal at the distant edges of this season. Propelled by wind and wave, unattached ice floes gouge and tear at the shoreline like thousands of berserk bulldozers. In one twenty-four-hour period in December of 1985, chunks of land extending fifty feet inland disappeared along some areas of the eastern coastline. Undermined lakefront homes crumbled and collapsed into the water.

In the natural world, this isn't a problem, it's just part of the normal process. In the world of the American native, who moved home and family wherever the seasons and natural conditions dictated, erosion was of little, if any, concern. To modern-day people, however, erosion is another of those irritants of the natural world to be controlled, stopped, or redirected and then ignored. But it doesn't work that way. Erosion has been a shaping force in the formation and alteration of Lake Michigan's shoreline since the glaciers last retreated to their northern breeding grounds.

It isn't that we haven't tried to control erosion. It's just that most of the currently used mechanisms work poorly, and redirect shore drift—affecting nearby property. The few mechanisms that do stop erosion, such as offshore concrete or steel barriers and shoreline concrete seawalls and riprap, are prohibitively expen-

sive and, in the words of William Ashworth in *The Late, Great Lakes,* are "ugly as hell."

Nature frequently exacts a heavy toll from those who ignore her direction and power, putting themselves in harm's way. This is exactly what happened when lake levels rose rapidly between 1982 and 1986, exacerbating shoreline erosion, destroying homes, and threatening entire neighborhoods. A great hue and cry went up from the coastal communities—some asked, some demanded—for their government to put an end to this destruction. Drain the lake into submission!

But a hue and cry had already gone up in the 1920s from the lake states and Canada. At that time, increasing water diversions through the Chicago River were being protested. It was a time of drought. Don't drain our lakes! Agreements were made, lawsuits were begun. In 1967, the U.S. Supreme Court set the maximum allowable diversion through the Chicago River at 3,200 cubic feet per second.

As the waters rose, and shorelines seemed to sink, all manner of diversion schemes were hatched, studies and research were begun, and truths that should have been self-evident were brought to light. Evaluation of the hydrology of Lake Michigan by environmental researchers and hydrologists, using weather logs and lake level historical data, showed the human ability to alter Great Lakes water levels to be less than previously believed.

The volume of water in Lake Michigan, compared to the size of its two outlets (the Straits of Mackinac and the Chicago River diversion), is huge. The lion's share of this water enters as precipitation, 80 percent of which leaves the lake again—not through any divertable outlet, but through the intractable process of large-scale evaporation. The only rational possibility of increased diversion was through the Chicago River—a river sacrificed to sewer status in 1900, when its flow into Lake Michigan was reversed, sending Chicago's sewage bobbing towards the Mississippi River. But even if outflow through the Chicago diversion were tripled, the lake would drop only one inch in six months. This miniscule magnitude was wholly inadequate in the face of an inland sea rising rapidly, not in inches but in feet.

This was unwelcome information to lakeshore residents with property in peril of shipping out to sea. We have grown accustomed to having our way with the natural world. Hills and mountains in the "wrong" place are leveled; unwanted wetlands are filled; the extremes of summer and winter are ignored as we live synthetic lives in hermetically sealed boxes. How in technology's name could an inland freshwater lake, not even an ocean, be so uncontrollable? But it was, and is.

If it was uncontrollable, it was equally unpredictable. It continued to rise rapidly, peaking in October

A lake-effect snowstorm makes landfall at St. Joseph.

Propelled by wind and waves, ice floes tear at the shoreline. This excavation continues until a solid shelf of ice is formed along the shore.

23

The unhappy result of building too close to an unstable shore.

Beach nourishment—longshore currents carry the products of erosion to a new site, building this sandbar and point at Point Beach State Forest.

North Bar Lake is an embayment lake near Sleeping Bear Dunes.

1986 at the highest lake level of the 20th century. (Lake levels have been both much higher and much lower in preceding centuries.) And then, unexpectedly, rapidly, and without human prediction, the lake dropped. By January 1987, in less than four months, water levels plummeted nearly a foot. As levels continued to fall by one-half to one foot per year through July 1989, concerns turned from erosion and shoreline protection to harbor and channel dredging, in the face of increasingly shallow waterways.

Calls for increased water diversion from Lake Michigan through the Chicago River continued, but from different sources. Residents of the arid West and Mississippi River shipping interests, all suffering from the droughts of the late 1980s, called for increased water from Lake Michigan. Shoreline property owners who originally called (sometimes angrily) for increased diversion to lower lake levels were, by August 1988, opposing efforts to increase the outflow of Lake Michigan into the Chicago River.

Shoreline property prices that had plummeted a few years previous began climbing rapidly. The heartbreak of homes falling into the lake, along with the newfound knowledge that the process of rising and falling lake levels is beyond reasonable human control, seemed to have been largely forgotten. Hardly the scenario of a species in control of its environment, or of itself.

The natural process of erosion continues, to greater and lesser degrees, regardless of lake levels. It always has and always will. But what is removed is always put back—someplace else. Sand plucked from the shores is carried by offshore currents, the force of waves falling back from shore, and by longshore currents flowing parallel to shore. When these movements are impeded and slowed by underwater or shoreline obstructions, they drop their loads of sand—creating spits and bars, extending beaches, and filling in or closing off bays.

Waves remove shoreline, only to give it to currents that create new and different shores. Something lost and something gained, the process continues. Residents and recreationists, happy recipients of the gain side of this equation, delight in the unique beauty of a host of embayment lakes: Silver, Crystal, Torch, Pentwater, Elk, Leelanau, Glen, Portage, Platte, Hamlin, Betsie, and Lake Charlevoix. Each of these lakes is a gift of the flip side of erosion—beach nourishment. As sands were carried by longshore currents, shore drift extended spits and built up bars that eventually closed off bays. This was the birth process of the numerous lakes along Lake Michigan's eastern shore, all the happy result of previous "current" events.

The longshore currents that manifest themselves in shoreline rearrangement are but one part of a complicated set of prevailing surface currents that whirl and flow about Lake Michigan. These currents, parented by prevailing winds (and, to a lesser degree, by the Coriolis force), are complex beyond the scope of this book. However, a few generalizations can be made. Along both east and west coasts, longshore currents flow northerly when pushed by southerly winds, and vice versa. In the open lake are two somewhat separate and circular currents, one in the south basin and one in the north basin. Currents in the south basin swirl generally counterclockwise—except in winter with northerly winds, when the rotation reverses to clockwise. Open lake currents of the north basin operate in a similar, but considerably more complex, pattern, including a swirl around the Beaver Island archipelago.

The enormity of Lake Michigan makes it subject to forces not normally associated with lakes. Its mass is sufficiently large to make it subject to lunar gravity, resulting in a tide. However, this Lilliputian tide is measured in inches, and generally goes unnoticed.

In contrast, the effect of changing weather conditions on the lake do not escape notice. Strong winds push water ahead of them, raising the water level on lee shores. Closely spaced barometric high- and low-pressure centers moving across Lake Michigan also have a tilting effect on the lake surface. When either of these water-tilting forces ceases, a surge of returning water moves from the high-level side of the lake to the lower side. Once set in motion, this surge continues moving back and forth across the lake, periodically raising and lowering the shoreline levels until its energy is spent. Termed "seiches," these surges vary in magnitude from inches to several feet, and in duration from hours to several days. More than once, while setting up camera and tripod near the water's edge, we have watched our shoreline subject disappear into a seiche, not to be seen again that day.

Not all seiches pass so innocuously. On April 7, 1983, a seiche sloshed back and forth between St. Joseph and Chicago. At St. Joseph, it was measured at four feet, and traveled inland seven hundred feet beyond the high-water mark. Chicago experienced a surge of nearly six feet, tearing ships from their moorings and tossing them against each other. Fortunately, this seiche occurred around half past one in the morning, and no one was injured. The seiche that hit Chicago on June 26, 1954 traveled rapidly at a height of ten feet, drowning seven people on a Chicago dock.

These up-and-down whims of an inland sea serve as humbling reminders to those who will heed them—the lake will not be trifled with, nor long ignored. This fact is indelibly etched in the consciousness of any sailor who has run for safe harbor on the leading

The St. Joseph North Pier Lights awash in heavy seas from a driving northwest wind.

edge of a fall storm. Lying, according to the *United States Coast Pilot*, "in the midst of a climatological battlefield" where the three major air masses of the North American continent collide, the Great Lakes are usually recipients of weather imported from other areas.

Spring and fall are the times of greatest warfare between these weather systems. But autumn is when the lake decides to become an active participant. When low-pressure systems meet the stored heat energy of the lake, they are often intensified into homegrown storms that would curl the hair of even the most hard-bitten saltwater sailors. This is the season that claimed the 17th century cargoship *Griffon,* and snapped the steel-hulled freighter *Bradley*'s back in 1958. It is the season that has littered the lake with countless broken hulks, many of which appear and disappear in the shifting sands along the shore.

Fall is also a season of fast-moving, hard-hitting squall lines. These brief but intense storms are created when a large and rapidly moving high-pressure air mass slams into the localized warm air mass (low-pressure system) over the lake. Cold, dense air spills over the top of the cold front and plummets down into the warm lake air, spawning a line of thunderstorms and severe winds.

Camping at Sleeping Bear Dunes one October, we watched one of these wild storms race across the lake. A listless gray sky greeted us that morning, and we were tempted to roll over and go back to sleep. But, having learned that gray skies often mask the serendipitous, we drove to a favorite shoreline overlook for breakfast. Sure enough, before we had taken the first bite of cereal, lightning flickered over the lake.

Out of the gray nothing, a rolling squall line spread across the horizon. Layered clouds—alternating blue steel-gray, near black, and dirty white—rolled and braided as they raced directly toward us. Lightning crackled repeatedly, striking the lake all along the squall line. It split the sky again and again over Sleeping Bear Point. Unable to reach waterspout status, whirlwinds kicked up spray and skimmed across the horizon. The water went black and the storm hit—hard. Wind shook our little camper, and the outside world disappeared as marble-sized hail banged, popped, and clattered all around. Hail fell harder and harder until it was one continuous deafening clatter.

And then it was over. From beginning to end, the

Lightning in a squall line heads for Sleeping Bear Dunes National Lakeshore.

A chinook salmon dies on the shore. These salmon have suffered increasing mortality due to Bacterial Kidney Disease (BKD). Although the exact cause of the chinook's increasing susceptibility to BKD is uncertain, some researchers suspect a link with the immune suppression capabilities of the many toxic wastes in this area.

A small, localized algal bloom near North Manitou Island.

whole process took less than half an hour. Mist drifted down out of the pines and filled the dune valleys. The feral beauty of the storm had passed; evidence of its brief life lay melting on the ground, in a suddenly wintry landscape of hailstones. But evidence of its passing also lay indelibly pressed in our memories, for the storm had blown some of its wild vitality into us that morning.

The transitional weather seasons of spring and fall bring dramatic storms to Lake Michigan; however, these seasons also bring less obvious, but equally significant, changes beneath the lake's surface. Much like its close cousin the wind, lake water moves not only laterally, but vertically as well. Quirky stuff water. Like the wind, it is one of the most yielding and yet most powerful of forces. Contracting as it cools, like air and most other substances, water becomes more dense. But here the comparison breaks down. This increasing density continues until water reaches the watershed temperature of 39.1 degrees Fahrenheit; at this point it does an abrupt about-face and begins gradually expanding. Slow expansion continues until water, reaching the freezing point, expands suddenly by nearly 10

percent in volume, and begins changing from the liquid state to the solid state. This may seem like mundane grade-school science, but it is of more than passing interest if you're a fish, or fishing enthusiast. It is precisely this density reversal that is responsible for the oxygen-distributing spring and fall turnovers.

In winter, surface water and floating ice, in their expanded state, are lighter than deeper, denser waters, which remain at about 40 degrees Fahrenheit. As the icy lake surface is warmed in springtime, its waters become heavier and sink, while warmer waters rise from the depths. For a while following this spring turnover, lake waters are generally the same temperature and density. This spring circulation allows some oxygen to move into deeper water.

With the heat of summer, the lake surface grows warmer and less dense, while deeper waters remain cold and heavy; the water stratifies into a warmer surface layer called the epilimnion, and a cool deeper layer, the hypolimnion. The transitional zone of interface between warm and cold water is called the thermocline. As summer continues, this stratification becomes more pronounced, inhibiting mixture of oxygen-rich epilimnion water with the oxygen-poor hypolimnion.

Autumn air temperatures cool the oxygen-rich surface water, which becomes denser and sinks as now comparatively warmer deep water rises. This fall turnover is an event of singular importance to the deepwater life systems in the lake. Without this autumn infusion of oxygen, life in the deep would nearly cease — zooplankton and phytoplankton levels would drop, and *Mysis relicta* (freshwater shrimp) would cease their up-and-down nocturnal journeys. The effects would ripple up the food chain to the very top fish, such as trout and salmon, that frequently cruise the deep, dependent on these lower food-chain organisms. And fish need all the help they can get, for they've had a tough go of it since modern humans muddied the waters.

LAKE ECOLOGY

Lake Michigan is young. It came into being but a geological yesterday, resulting in an ecologic system of comparative youth and simplicity. There was a time, as recently as two hundred years ago, when this infant was growing strong and healthy. Its life systems were expanding and slowly diversifying, but, because of their youth and limited diversity, they were highly dependent on each other and very sensitive to rapid changes.

One hundred eighty species of fish motored through the waters of this glacial progeny: burbot, whitefish, lake trout, walleye, menominee, pike, pickerel, herring, sculpin, and sturgeon, to name but a few. They spawned in bays and river mouths, and the shallows often boiled with their activity.

Sturgeon — now there's a fish. Blessed with a face only a mother sturgeon could love, this magnificent beast was symbolic of the lake that spawned it: enormous, unique, and sensitive to change. Huge by any standard (up to nine feet in length and four hundred pounds in weight), a sturgeon's potential life span was as much as 150 years. Such longevity was a near necessity for a fish that took its own sweet time to reproduce itself. Not maturing sexually until age twenty to twenty-five, sturgeon then spawn at the leisurely rate of once every five years, taking several months to finish laying a few eggs here and a few eggs there. For these reasons the sturgeon, like its ecosystem, was (and is) very sensitive to rapid changes in its environment.

To understand the story of fish in Lake Michigan is to understand the history of recent human activity in that lake's basin. All the environmental and ecological horrors perpetrated in the misbegotten name of "progress" throughout the Lake Michigan Basin have, in one way or another, been instrumental in destabilizing life in the lake.

It is important to point out that no one set out purposely to destroy the lake ecology, to kill and contaminate the fish. But such ecological blunders are the normal by-product of a mentality that sees humans as all-important, and considers the rest of the natural world as expendable. The Native American mind viewed itself as part of the natural world, and subject to its laws and limits. The collective European attitude that flowed in from the East Coast, surging over the lake's basin like a tidal wave in the 1800s, viewed the natural world as a possession, to be used in any way the newcomers saw fit.

The first large-scale blow to the lake's ecology came with the logging boom that flourished in the second half of the 19th century. Nearly every stream and river was choked with logs en route to the lumber mills near the lake. These logs gouged and scraped river bottoms and banks, destroying vegetation and spreading sediments over spawning beds. Lumber mills dumped massive volumes of sawdust into rivers and bays, further smothering spawning grounds. Some rivers, such as the Milwaukee River, were so choked with sawdust that lake fish were physically unable to enter to spawn.

By the early 1900s, the North Woods were gone. And so was the forest's protective effect. Without this magnificent buffer, barren lands eroded, further covering spawning grounds with sediment. Gone too was the forest's cooling effect on run-off water. Streams, rivers, and bays became warmer. Cool-water fish (whitefish, lake trout, and others) found the warmer waters less desirable for spawning. The stage was being prepared for destabilizing exotic species yet to come, species preferring warmer spawning waters. The huge fires that for years consumed discarded timber slashings left their legacy in the lake; lye formed when ash-laden run-off entered the waters, degrading aquatic vegetation and killing huge numbers of fish.

With the logging boom came settlement of Lake Michigan's coastline — and the beginning of the second big blow to lake ecology, one that continues to hammer at the lake. Lake Michigan was treated like a large sewer and refuse dump. As lakeshore communities and industries increased in size and number, they continued to dump increasing volumes of sewage, industrial wastes, and agricultural run-off into the lake. Decomposition of this mess required increasingly huge amounts of dissolved oxygen — oxygen that should have passed through the collective gills of an already stressed fish population.

To make matters worse, nutrients in this discarded glop fueled a boom in algae populations. Algal blooms were not a new phenomenon; algal bloom, after all, was credited with giving Green Bay its name. However, these blooms had previously been an occasional happening in a few shallow areas of the lake. They were now becoming frequent, leaving a stinking slimy mess on many beaches.

What algal blooms did below water was equally disgusting. The short-lived, but rapidly reproducing, algae showered the depths with a continuous rain of dead and decaying cells. Biological oxygen demand in the lake shot sky-high. This was an especially concentrated problem in near-shore and shallow areas during the spring and early summer spawning season, due to a Great Lakes phenomenon known as the "thermal bar." Early in the season, shallow waters near shore warm rapidly, forming a vertical thermocline-like thermal bar that separates warm near-shore water circulation from the colder open-lake waters. With pollution discharge and algal bloom held near shore, in the prime fish-breeding zone, life in the lake was pushed even closer to total collapse.

And then there was commercial fishing, often blamed for the decline in fish populations. This is only partly true. The decline was, in large part, due to the litany of human-induced environmental degradations. It is valid to question if commercial fishing would have been so destructive in an unstressed and healthy fish ecology. But the question is moot. Just as the lake's life support systems were reeling from repeated blows, commercial fishing technology became more and more efficient.

Re-enter the sturgeon. These endearingly homely fish had been considered trash fish. They were killed and tossed out of nets, stacked in huge piles, and burned onshore. And then society changed its mind, and its tastes. Sturgeon caviar became the new sensation. In addition, sturgeon swim bladders were found to produce a gelatin that made superb isinglass for carriage windows. In 1880, over 4 million pounds of these previously disliked and discarded fish were harvested from Lake Michigan. By 1900, only 140,000 pounds were brought to market, and sturgeon were brought to near extinction. To this day, this remarkable laid-back fish is a rarity in the lake.

Enter the exotics. For thousands of years, life in the lake underwent gradual change, adapting and evolving at a leisurely pace. All of this changed abruptly with the new species introduced by human activity—some intentionally, many unintentionally.

In the late 19th century, European immigrants brought carp to the Lake Michigan area, to raise for food in Wisconsin farm ponds. These fish spawn in mud; those that escaped the ponds and reached Lake Michigan thrived in the sediment-laden streams that had become poor spawning grounds for other fish species.

Many unsuccessful attempts were made in the late 1800s to plant salmon in Lake Michigan. Even today, the salmon that cruise the lake are primarily hatchery-raised and stocked annually. Salmon are anadromous fish, that normally live in salt water but swim up freshwater streams to spawn. As with a few other anadromous fish (lampreys, alewives, and smelt), salmon are also capable of living out their entire life cycle in fresh water, something the native Atlantic salmon had done for many years in Lake Ontario until they became extinct in that lake in 1898.

In 1912, salmon were planted in Crystal Lake, one of the many embayment lakes of the eastern shore. The salmon perished, but smelt, planted thoughtfully with the salmon as a food fish, thrived. Smelt made it to Lake Michigan, where their populations virtually exploded. This was bad news and good news. On the one hand, smelt compete well with whitefish and herring, and the smelt population has often swelled and collapsed in inverse proportions to herring populations. On the other hand, the smelt was a commercial and sportfishing success. To this day, smelt is one of the most commercially viable fish. Lake Michigan residents flock to spawning streams and dip out phenomenal numbers of this newcomer every spring. Some towns have celebrated the smelt with festivals, including such activities as smelt wrestling (much like mud wrestling, with dead smelt replacing the mud—an exercise in olfactory masochism).

Meanwhile, much more ominous and devastating newcomers were swimming and wriggling up the Great Lakes chain, one just ahead of the other. The eel-like sea lamprey came first. Its anadromous drive always to swim upstream propelled it up the Hudson River and then into the Erie Canal at Troy, New York. For reasons known only to lampreys (and later alewives), they made a hard right at Oswego, New York, and passed through the Oswego Canal into Lake Ontario; they may have also beelined directly up the St. Lawrence River to Lake Ontario. There lampreys were first seen in 1835, and alewives in the 1860s. They remained in Lake Ontario until changes in the Welland Canal in 1919 allowed them to take this Niagara Falls bypass. Once into Lake Erie, it was only a matter of time until they arrived in all the other lakes.

The lamprey slithered through the Straits of Mackinac and was first noted in Lake Michigan in 1936. Here it found a lake that had been inadvertently prepared for its successful arrival. Lake Michigan had many streams available for lamprey spawning; even more fortuitous (from the lamprey point of view) was the increased temperature of these streams, created by the North Woods' demise. Lampreys prefer warm spawning streams; trout do not. Lampreys began voraciously parasitizing lake trout, destroying as much as 5 million pounds of fish annually. The commercial catch plummeted from over 6½ million pounds in 1943 to 4,000 pounds in 1952. Lamprey then turned

A few commercial fishing enterprises still survive. Here the Shirley K. *brings her catch to home port, St. James on Beaver Island.*

Small die-offs of alewives still show up on beaches in spring and early summer.

Lake Michigan's industrialized south shore has been referred to as "The Sulfur Capital of the World."

to whitefish, herring, walleye, and perch.

Alewives motored into Lake Michigan in 1949, with impeccable timing. Once again, one disaster had prepared the way for the next. With the decimation of lake trout, alewives entered a lake devoid of any serious predator. By the middle 1960s, alewives made up 90 percent of Lake Michigan's fish, by weight. All of this brings us right back to the worsening algal bloom problem. Although started by increased pollution and nutrient excess in the lake, the algae problem was magnified many times over by the exploding alewife populations. One of the checks and balances on algae is a group of small animals called zooplankton, which use algae as a main food source. Unfortunately, alewives were gorging themselves on zooplankton. The inevitable equation: more alewives equals less zooplankton equals more algae.

With rampant pollution and the arrival of unwanted exotic species, the lake ecology had become a dreadful mess. According to Dr. Jim Kitchell, of the Limnology Lab at the University of Wisconsin, "In the 1940s and '50s, Green Bay was an abysmal place. Fishes simply wouldn't live in the lower end of Green Bay and the Fox River."

By the middle 1960s, the lake was completely unstable. Water quality was awful. Alewives proliferated

ridiculously, culminating in a late winter die-off in 1966–67 that left a spring shoreline littered with dead and decaying alewives, piled three feet high and twenty feet wide all around the southern end of the lake.

Similar ecological blunders had been made throughout the nation, creating a national water-quality crisis. Things had to change. And with the U.S. Clean Water Act of 1972, things eventually did improve. Sewage systems were upgraded, industrial discharges into streams were reduced. In addition, the lamprey had been found to have a chink in its armor. In 1958, the lampricide TFM was discovered, and treatment of Lake Michigan spawning streams began in 1960. Within a few years, sea lamprey populations dropped dramatically, and continued stream treatment has kept them low. Improved and intensive stocking of salmon (chinook and coho) and trout (rainbow, steelhead, and brown) was more successful in the late 1960s. These fish began mopping up the alewives. Fewer alewives were left to consume zooplankton, leaving more zooplankton to eat more algae. Water quality improved tremendously, and once again the lake was alive with fish.

Lampreys and alewives still swim in the lake, although in much reduced numbers. The stocked salmon and trout have spawned such a boom in sportfishing that continued intensive restocking programs are required to keep up with demand. (The Great Lakes Commission estimated that this industry, in 1985, brought in over $331 million to the Lake Michigan Basin!) Life in the lake has improved greatly in the last twenty-five to thirty years.

However, new exotics are coming; most are carried in the ballast tanks of ocean-going ships. When ships empty these ballast tanks to compensate for the reduced flotation of fresh water, or to take on Great Lakes cargo, the lake is inoculated with whatever organisms were included in the saltwater ballast.

Zebra mussels have been seen on a ship's hull in Green Bay. Already these exotic mollusks have begun causing phenomenally expensive obstructions in public water- and power-plant intakes in Lakes Erie and Ontario. In what unknown ways will they impact on lake ecology? And what about the spiny water flea, *Bythotrephes cederstroemi* (also referred to as B.C.)? Just recently gaining a foothold throughout the lakes, it provides many fish diets with particularly low-quality nutrition, while competing by feeding on the same zooplankton that small larval fish feed on. And then there is the European river ruffe, described by Marg Dochoda, fishery biologist for the Great Lakes Fishery Commission, as a "spiny awful little fish." This exotic member of the perch family reproduces rapidly, and has an insatiable appetite for other fish species' eggs. It has been seen in Duluth harbor, Lake Superior; if previous experiences hold, it's coming our way. And even flounders are occasionally seen, "both left-eyed and right-eyed." The list goes on. What will all these newcomers mean to a just recovering lake ecology?

Enter the microcontaminants, that insidious parade of toxins, carcinogens, and mutagens with which our modern world has imperiled itself: DDT, lead, cadmium, toxaphene, chlordane, PCBs—the list goes on. According to the Lake Michigan Federation, "about 300 toxic chemicals and heavy metals have been discovered in the water, in sediments, or in fish from the lake."

For a long time, industries dumped their discarded chemical wastes directly into streams, rivers, and the lake itself. Sewage treatment plants did the same, with minimal (if any) standards for nonhuman waste disposal. These point sources are the most obvious and easily regulated toxic chemical sources. With increasing state and federal regulations, point-source contamination, while still a problem, has been markedly reduced.

Non-point-source contamination is another matter entirely. As much as 57 percent of Lake Michigan's annual load of PCBs now comes from the atmosphere, in contaminated precipitation and dry deposition. Of the lake's annual dose of lead, 99.5 percent is airborne. An assortment of harmful chemicals also enters the lake from leaking storage facilities and dumps, carried by run-off and contaminated ground water.

Perhaps the most pernicious non-point sources are the contaminated and toxic sediments at the bottom of many harbors, streams, and rivers. Here is where an already complex problem gets completely out of hand. While every one of the mentioned sources contributes to the worsening toxic sediment conundrum, the sediments themselves have become a source for the entrance of toxics into the lake's life cycles. Much like the exotic life forms that have irreversibly impacted the lake's ecology, once hazardous wastes are introduced into the system, they take on a life of their own—becoming virtually impossible to remove.

Out of hundreds of such contaminants, let's look at just one of the current worrisome pollutants cycling and recycling through life systems in the lake: PCBs. PCBs (polychlorinated biphenyls) are a group of colorless and odorless chemicals first produced commercially in the late 1920s. Phenomenally durable (requiring in excess of 2,000 degrees Fahrenheit to reliably destroy them), they gained wide use in electrical insulators, inks, hydraulic and heat transfer fluids, lubricants, and many other industrial applications. It is appropriate to discuss PCBs in the plural. Based on two modified benzene rings with two or more chlorine atoms attached, there are 209 kinds (congeners) of PCBs, each with a unique toxicity.

Beginning in the 1950s, large volumes of PCBs were being used, with PCB-laden wastes discharged directly into one river and stream after another. PCBs were believed to be inert; everyone thought they were harmless. That they are anything but harmless was proved in 1968, when a heat exchanger leaked PCBs into rice oil, which was later consumed by 1,200 unsuspecting Japanese. The resulting symptoms ranged from skin lesions to blindness and birth abnormalities—and five deaths. The severity of symptoms correlated with the amount of contaminated rice oil ingested. According to ecologist Dr. Jim Ludwig, "A few years later this grisly experiment was repeated in Taiwan in another cooking oil contamination incident. Children born to contaminated mothers were horribly damaged, more likely to become sick, less intelligent, and with many lesions."

Meanwhile, PCBs continued to be discharged into waters throughout the industrialized world, including Lake Michigan. Animal studies pointed to evidence of PCB-introduced cancer, immune suppression, and a host of toxic ills. By the middle 1970s, PCBs were "banned" in the United States. But it was too late; a chemical Pandora's box had already loosed its furies on the environment, and there was no putting them back.

So here we are, stuck in the muck—and a very toxic muck it is. Sediments from some areas of Waukegan harbor have shown 500,000 parts per million (ppm) PCBs—that's 50 percent PCBs! Toxic sediments in the Grand Calumet River/Indiana Harbor Canal go ten feet deep in many areas. Similar problems exist in nearly every industrial harbor throughout the Great Lakes (throughout the world, for that matter).

Unfortunately, these sediments do not stay in place. Stirred up and moved by shipping traffic, currents, waves, and bottom-feeding organisms, they continue to enter the lake. Ten thousand tons of contaminated Indiana Harbor sediments enter the lake each year. The tons of PCBs in the Kalamazoo River are estimated to contribute 240 pounds of PCBs to the lake yearly. Out of sight may be out of mind, but it is not out of the system.

But hasn't lake water so diluted these contaminants that we are not really at any risk? This is the thinking behind the trite and trivializing slogan, "Dilution is the solution to pollution." Don't believe it. The wild card is something called bioconcentration and biomagnification. PCBs, and many other chlorinated hydrocarbons, have an affinity for lipids (body fats); consequently, continued modest consumption of such chemicals results in increasing concentrations stored in fat cells. In the lake, PCBs attach to minute particles, which are ingested by the smallest life forms. These are eaten by larger life forms, and on up the food chain—biomagnifying with each step. By the time PCBs reach top-of-the-food-chain animals such as large game fish, raptors, gulls, terns, cormorants, mink, and otter, they have been concentrated many times over—until, in the words of wildlife ecologist Dr. Jim Ludwig, "In order to get an equivalent dose to one salmon meal, you'd have to drink all your water for five hundred years from the lake."

Compounding all of this is recent evidence suggesting that PCBs, once in the lake's life systems, do not remain in their original proportions. The original PCB discharges contained a mix of differently chlorinated PCBs; this mix has long been thought to stay the same as it moves through the food chain. According to Dr. Ludwig, new findings confirm that the more toxic PCBs (those with four to six chlorinations) are being concentrated in the fat cells of living beings. In Dr. Ludwig's words: "What we're ending up with is that a part per million PCB in a cormorant egg (or lake trout) is actually six to ten times more toxic than the originally discharged PCB to the water."

This is not just a hypothetical toxicity. Fish sprout tumors. Gulls, terns, and double-crested cormorants exhibit a host of abnormalities, including reproductive impairment, club feet, crossed bills, and other birth defects. Mink and otter populations have been so decimated by reproductive impairment that they have been virtually extirpated from the lake's basin.

Humans who consume the larger game fish are not without risk. Since the 1970s, the strong association between PCB ingestion and human cancer has prompted the Food and Drug Administration (F.D.A.) and every state around the lake to issue cautions and recommended limits on fish consumption. Nearly five pages of the 1989 Michigan Fishing Guide are given to the potential risks of various kinds and sizes of fishes, and the safest way to clean and prepare them. The University of Wisconsin Sea Grant Institute distributes a paper entitled "Eating Lake Michigan Fish," dealing entirely with PCBs in fish, cautions and recommendations on which fish to avoid, and the safest way to clean and prepare fish. And now we learn that studies of infants whose mothers regularly consumed modest amounts of Lake Michigan fish have found subtle but consistent birth, developmental, behavioral, and memory deficits (similar to the abnormalities found in infants of mothers accidentally exposed to PCBs in Japan and Taiwan).

All of this from PCBs—just one of the estimated three hundred dangerous chemicals in the lake. And every year nearly six hundred *new* chemicals are produced, or used, in the Great Lakes Basin. Is this the better tomorrow that the proponents of unrestricted industry and technology have been promising us?

It is important to understand that the degradation of the Lake Michigan Basin is, to greater and lesser extents, what has happened the world over. There is no escaping responsibility for our species's mistakes. There is no place to hide. And yet, Lake Michigan is still a lake of exquisite beauty and vitality. It, like its four sisters, is a lake in peril—but not lost. Indeed, hopeful glimmerings, but just glimmerings, peek over the environmental horizon.

Perhaps the most hopeful and necessary prelude to real improvement is public awareness. Organizations such as Lake Michigan Federation, Great Lakes United, Center for the Great Lakes, Sierra Club, National Wildlife Federation, National Audubon Society, and a whole host of other regional, state, and local environmental citizen groups are the niduses around which critically important public action has crystallized.

In 1972, Canada and the United States signed the Great Lakes Water Quality Agreement, which committed both nations to cleaning up the Great Lakes. Considerable progress was made, but the agreement was too narrow in scope. In 1978, the agreement was renegotiated, emphasizing an "ecosystem approach" and the need for "zero discharge" of "persistent toxic substances." This was an event of immense

The bioaccumulation of toxic wastes in large game fish is a threat to Lake Michigan sportfishing, a popular recreation and a multimillion-dollar industry.

significance—the first time that governments had acknowledged, and put in writing, the importance of dealing with the environment as a whole system rather than as politically significant segments. It was the first time that governments agreed in writing to the necessity for zero discharge of persistent toxins.

Like so many other promising governmental contracts, this agreement met with less than enthusiastic implementation and enforcement. But, as is often the case, the public was ahead of its elected political leaders and began insisting that their governments fulfill their promises. In 1987, the Great Lakes Water Quality Agreement was again renegotiated. This time, the public was an active participant, as five environmental groups had input in the negotiations of the two nations. This new agreement set up specific mechanisms for identifying areas of concern (AOCs) and developing remedial action plans (RAPs) for these areas. It defined the ecosystem as "the interacting components of air, land, water, and living organisms, including humans." It also promised a continued partnership with the public. In 1989, Great Lakes citizens voiced their concerns, in more than two days of public forums at the International Joint Commission Biennial Meeting,

described by Great Lakes United as "the first biennial meeting of the *people* of the Great Lakes." If we are to make any real and continuous progress, we must all stay alert and involved.

Reflecting on all that has happened, and is still happening, it is easy to become discouraged and depressed. But there is cause for hope. Where appropriate regulatory action has been enforced, signs of improvement have begun to show up.

Since DDT was banned in 1972, its presence in lake trout has steadily declined. According to Dr. Harold Humphrey, an epidemiologist with the Michigan Department of Public Health, "The bottom line is, ten years ago you had double digit values for PCBs, of 18 to 20 parts per million in lake trout. Today you get single digit values. Some small younger trout actually pass the F.D.A. guideline of 2 ppm; larger, older ones do not, but they're not at 20 ppm like they were. They're more like 7 to 9 ppm. The same has held with salmon—chinook and coho."

Dr. David Devault, of the Environmental Protection Agency's Great Lakes National Program Office, confirms the decline in DDT and PCBs, but cautions, "The downside is that it looks like the decline has leveled out." DDT and PCBs are still used in other countries, and are carried by global winds. The concern voiced by many experts is that we may have reached an equilibrium—especially with PCBs—where these toxic contaminants follow the hydrologic cycle.

But what is the effect of these decreased concentrations on living organisms? One of the best studies linking PCBs with adverse effects on living organisms in Lake Michigan was a study of Forster's terns in 1983. This study showed a strong link between reproductive impairment and dietary exposure to PCBs in Forster's terns. Five years later, a repeat study of the same tern colonies has yielded encouraging initial findings. Discussing the field data, Dr. H. J. Harris (one of the principal investigators in both studies) is cautiously optimistic: "The field data says the terns are reproducing normally. The incubation times were normal. The hatching rates were very high. I think that's encouraging." Laboratory analysis from the repeat study yielded somewhat more "perplexing" results. Although a few of the results showed no change in toxic activity, there was "a lower percentage of toxic congeners present, a reduction in actual concentration of congener 126" (one of the more toxic forms of PCB).

Dr. Harris, in preparing a "State of the Bay Report" for the Green Bay area, expressed even more reason for encouragement: "I know how tough these problems are. But most of the facts, as far as trends are concerned, point towards improved resources." He points to the return of wild celery, an important food for waterfowl, especially canvasback ducks, and to the marked reduction in discharge of hazardous effluents from the bay's public sewage treatment plants.

For the first time in a long time, many researchers are expressing cautious optimism. According to Dr. Kitchell, people are disturbed that fish in the Fox River and Green Bay have tumors. But this is an improvement. In the 1960s and 1970s, fish were unable to survive in this area! It's a strange irony that we are reduced to celebrating fish with tumors.

There are some important conclusions to be drawn from all this. Contrary to the popular saying, what we don't know *can* indeed hurt us. Even though we are beginning to see the dark at the end of a previously well-lit ecological tunnel—current problems and bad metaphors notwithstanding—all is not lost. The improvements seen recently are terribly inadequate if taken as endpoints, but when seen as initial steps in an increasing commitment to a healthy environmental system, they are tremendously encouraging. We do have the capacity to reverse the gradual shutting down of life systems in our world. The solution lies neither in ignoring the situation, nor in living without reasonable conveniences, nor in deteriorating into incapacitating depression. We still live in a resilient and wonderful environment.

Our forebears honestly believed Lake Michigan, and the rest of the world, were just too large and powerful to damage. Now we know better. Attitudes are beginning to change. Concern for the environment is no longer the personal passion of a few well-heeled liberals. (Indeed, it never was—this is a false image fostered by those who profit from our ecologic insensitivities.) Now, more than ever, preservation of the health and diversity of our natural world is of concern to everyone. We are just beginning to understand what Native Americans took as a matter of faith. In Chief Seattle's words, "The earth does not belong to man; man belongs to the earth. . . . All things are connected. Whatever befalls the earth befalls the sons of the earth. Man did not weave the web of life; he is merely a strand in it. Whatever he does to the web, he does to himself." Deteriorating environments lead to deteriorating life forms—all life forms, including humans.

Not only are we affected by what we eat, but also by what we drink and breathe. And, to a large extent, our spiritual and emotional health is determined by the health of our environment. This places the environmental movement in an entirely new light. In the preservation of our wild and natural environment is the preservation of our human future. And we do have the capacity to change our destructive course. What remains is to live in a respectful and responsible manner with the other life forms that have birthright to this planet. To do this requires that we take to heart the most basic and important tenet of the medical world, *Primum non nocere:* First do no harm.

THE NORTH WOODS

That land is a community is the basic concept of ecology, but that land is to be loved and respected is an extension of ethics.
— *Aldo Leopold*

The North Woods—these are the woods of birchbark canoes and Indians, of voyageurs and lumberjacks; the woods of myth and legend. How can the North Woods experience be translated to paper? It is emotions and aesthetics, ferns and fragrance, the beauty of gray March days with snow fog moving through the forest. It is the renewal of a fresh rain traveling along conifer needles to well up in clear fat droplets that fall heavily into the duff. And it is pipsissewa and bunchberry, ground pine and white pine. To enter the North Woods is to breathe deeply and be renewed as city tensions are shed like autumn leaves—replaced by a sense of belonging and continuity as we enter a time and place of moss and meaning.

The North Woods that border all but the most southwestern shores of Lake Michigan are a woods of transition. They are the southern edge of one of the world's great forests, one that changes into boreal forest as it marches on from the upper Great Lakes into northern Canada, where it meets the tundra. To the south, the North Woods fade away as plants characteristic of coniferous forests are replaced by those of the central hardwood forest.

The geographic line running from Milwaukee across Lake Michigan to the Holland/Muskegon area, then east to Saginaw Bay, generally follows the southern boundary of the North Woods (with the exception of a finger of increasingly diluted North Woods trailing southward along the eastern lakeshore, to approximately the Michigan border). The transition zone around this line where these two dissimilar forests give

way to each other is called the Tension Zone, a region of quiet botanical warfare. North of this zone, conifers are increasingly victorious. South of the zone, conifers are either completely absent, or so uncommon that their influence on the forest is insignificant. North of the Tension Zone, the growing season is shorter with fewer frost-free-days, the average annual daily minimum temperature and mean annual temperature are lower, and soil fertility and moisture-holding ability are lower. All these factors favor conifers. All these factors also affect human activity. North of the Tension Zone are fewer people, smaller towns, less *tension*.

The North Woods have been defined and delineated by different sources in different ways. We find the North Woods to have two basic characters— one tangible, the other intangible but no less real. The first character is the plant and animal community, dependent on the unique geologic, hydrologic, and meterologic characteristics of the area. The second, from a human perspective (and perhaps from the perspectives of some other life forms), is of an experiential, emotional, and spiritual nature, dependent on interaction with the still wild and natural dignity of the North Woods.

As the last glacier receded about 10,000 years ago, the boreal forest followed close on its heels, at an average rate of fifty miles per century. First came the sphagnum bogs and cedar swamps. Boreal forest followed, composed primarily of spruces and balsam fir, interspersed with birches and aspens. Finally came the

Bunchberry and club moss thrive only in undisturbed forests with a high percentage of conifers.

succession of plants in the North Woods that remains the dominant forest type around most of Lake Michigan today—the mixed hardwood forest. This is a misleading name. The trees distinguishing this forest from its southern neighbor are the conifers sprinkled among the northern hardwoods.

The North Woods today are the preferred home of two of our most magnificent conifers: hemlock and white pine. There was a time not so very long ago, in the mid-1800s, when much of this area was dominated by pines—especially the stately white pine and its sibling, the red pine. Sandy and gravelly soils left by the last glacier, which bulldozed the richest soils to Ohio, Indiana, and Illinois, were best suited to the growth of these pines.

And grow they did. When white people first entered the North Woods, the forest was dominated by pines throughout most of the area that would become Michigan and over one-half of present-day Wisconsin. This forest, known as "the edge of night" by the earliest white settlers, was a forest of quiet and brooding majesty. White pines with three-foot diameters were commonplace. Their pillarlike straight trunks lofted a verdant canopy one hundred feet and more above the footstep-absorbing duff of the forest floor.

The edge of night was also a forest of persistence and antiquity. Four times it was ground and bulldozed into southern regions, yet four times it refused to say "uncle" as it rode the glaciers' wake back to the north country. The North Woods' antiquity is a function not only of their persistent self-restoration but also of the ancientness of their flagship members, the pines. One of the first seed-bearing trees to evolve, pines were well established before the age of dinosaurs—and were a silent witness to the evolutionary arrival of mammals, deciduous trees, primates, and grasses.

Pines are such a successful design that they have flourished relatively unchanged for over 250 million years. Green needles minimize surface area and have a waxlike coating to minimize moisture loss in cold, or hot and dry, climates. Staying on the tree throughout the winter, evergreen needles are ready to function as soon as spring growth conditions arrive—a distinct advantage in the North Woods, where the frost-free season occasionally is little more than a memory. This short growing season, along with the relatively nutrient-poor North Woods soil of sand, gravel, and rock, affords little extravagance. In response, pines (and other conifers) conserve resources by holding new needles for three to five years, while constantly dropping older needles—resulting in a constant gentle rain of organic material to the forest floor.

Pines are simple and economical in their reproductive cycles: no flashy and sexy pistils and stamens, ovaries, or fruiting bodies; no reliance on flighty insects. Pines and other conifers go about their reproductive business with cones and windborne pollen. Two seeds are at the base of each woody scale of the cone; an upward scooplike curve allows pollen to land and slide down to the waiting seeds.

The persistence of pines has endured numerous geologic and meteorologic cataclysms. But the most recent upheavals in the North Woods have been the arrival of the ax and crosscut saw wielded by 19th century humans, and the bulldozers of 20th century developers. Not since the glaciers has such wholesale destruction been wreaked on the North Woods. Prior to the coming of the white wave from the Old World, Native Americans had caused relatively little damage to the forests, in spite of understory fires used for game management and agriculture. But after the "cut-and-run" logging boom of the 1800s, nearly all of the old growth was removed—leaving a desertlike landscape, clear-cut, stump-riddled, and burned-over.

Fires have always played a part in forest ecology. Lightning-caused fires cleared patches of forest at the approximate rate of one fire every thirty to fifty years. These understory fires little affected the fire-resistant trunks of white and red pines, and actually stimulated the opening of jack pine cones. The holocaust that followed logging was another matter altogether. With slash from limbs and treetops lying deep everywhere, the whole area was a tinderbox that was lit repeatedly. Forest fires were a near constant occurrence. In the face of such frequent and intense fires, all trees were burned repeatedly. This put conifers at a distinct disadvantage. Many hardwoods can send new shoots and suckers up from already established roots and stumps, but conifers have to wait for cones to open and seeds to germinate.

Little, if any, effort was made to put out these wide-ranging fires for two reasons: Humans had virtually no effective fire-fighting ability at that time in the face of such conflagrations; and, fires were seen as an efficient way to clear the decimated forest for agriculture. But fire has no judgment. It feeds blindly. Along with the slash went the forest floor—the duff that was the giant sponge of the North Woods. Without this sponge, rains carried away what little soil was present. And when it didn't rain, the barren soil dried up and baked. To add insult to shortsightedness, the North Woods' sandy and gravelly soils provided little nutrition for agricultural efforts. The logging boom came and went; the agricultural boom never did.

The North Woods are still rebounding from the logging days—so are human population levels. After the logging boom consumed itself, boom towns went bust; not long afterwards, agricultural expectations plummeted like water through sand. And the people left. They pocketed their hopes and dreams and headed

White pine are still returning to the North Woods (Nordhouse Dunes Wilderness Area).

The protective, absorbent duff of an undisturbed North Woods forest floor.

A morel mushroom is a prized find in the springtime mixed hardwood forest.

Dwarf lake iris, amid club moss, at the Ridges Sanctuary on the Door Peninsula.

south of the Tension Zone, seeking jobs in the cities and industries that were covering up the south shore of Lake Michigan.

The North Woods rested and then rose phoenix-like from the ashes. Colonies of aspens sprouted. Jack pines brought life back to the barren sands. The whole marvelous process of plant succession brought in the white and red pines, maples, beeches, and birches. The slow growth of cedars again filled the swamps. Black spruces again tiptoed onto floating sphagnum mats.

Today the pines persist, although drastically attenuated in size and numbers. While the pines were waiting for their cones to open and seeds to germinate, hardwoods were already out of the starting gate with stump and root shoots stretching skyward. As a result, the modern North Woods now have a much higher mix of hardwoods—maples, birches, aspens, and beeches.

With the return of the forest came a return of people. This time the axes and saws have been replaced by fishing rods and cameras. Every weekend, every holiday, and all summer long, the cities experience a mass exodus as people head to the North Woods for recreation.

Re-creation—that's a good word, and a good process. Modern race-pace city life, for all its seeming comforts, has fractured and fragmented our sense of belonging and continuity. The frenetic high-tech lifestyle that burst onto the scene in the last century has come as quite a shock to the human psyche—a psyche evolved over the millennia in an environment dominated by biological rhythms, natural smells and sounds, and botanical visions. And so we return to the North Woods, vaguely and hopefully aware that Thoreau was onto something of elemental importance when he penned "in Wildness is the preservation of the World."

The renewal of emotional and spiritual health that often takes place in the forest also allows the return of a healthy sense of humor. And a good sense of humor is a near necessity in the spring, when the "morelly" deficient start roaming the woods. Morels are popularly considered *the* edible wild mushroom. When "oak leaves are the size of squirrels' ears," when hepatica blossoms are beginning to fade and Dutchman's-breeches and trilliums are bright white, morel time has arrived. Parked cars are found along every backroad; their owners scan the area to insure secrecy of favorite morel grounds, before disappearing into the woods, hopes high and collecting bags in hand.

The appearance of these fungal delights seems to turn normally sober and prudent people into grinning liars. Tall tales surface every spring—of mammoth morels snaked out of the woods with Jeeps and logging chains, and of morel rustlers with chainsaws.

But for many people, morel hunting, like deer hunting, is an excuse to spend time in the woods. The low-angled sunlight of spring filters through pastel infant leaves, and the clean fresh smell of woodland humus mixes with the aroma of wild leeks as we venture into the birth/rebirth that is spring.

Spring's renewal brings a profusion of color to the forest floor in an array of delicate shadings: the soft yellow of trout lilies; pale lavender hepatica; blue, white, and yellow violets; and the happy little pink and white faces of spring beauties. But the flower that says "spring" in the North Woods, more than any other, is the trillium. Requiring a minimum of six years before flowering, and a rich, moist, undisturbed humus, this wild member of the lily family is a good barometer of the health of a forest. There are still areas of the North Woods where a springtime wave of white trilliums surges across the forest floor.

Meanwhile a quiet little event is taking place at the north end of the lake. The sun-loving dwarf lake iris opens its petals along near-shore forest edges and small woodland openings. In the entire world, these state- and federally-protected miniature irises are known to thrive only in a few unmolested areas at the north end of Lakes Michigan and Huron. However, where they are found, their colonies spread luxuriantly over the ground.

But spring is a fleeting season. Soon trilliums age to lavender and fade away. Bunchberry blossoms and gaywings, having trailed spring into early June, give way as summer comes in—green and robust, full of life and comfort. Released from the tensions of hunting season and from the threat of winter starvation, deer munch contentedly on their summer salads of grasses, forbs, and other leafy plants. And the rolling auditory signature of pileated woodpeckers is once again joined by the collective territorial voice of a multitude of returning songbirds. Especially welcome are the northern (Baltimore) orioles, so important in controlling the cyclical seven-to-ten-year explosion of tent caterpillar populations.

This is also the prime season for human migration, as thousands of stressed souls return to the cool serenity of the North Woods. More than a few small towns, still suffering from the crash of the logging boom, have staked their hopes on becoming vacationing tourist boom towns. Some of them have succeeded.

As the summer matures, bunchberry justifies its name by producing fistfuls of red berries that insist on being seen among the shining club moss. And wood ducks, who look like they have been painted by a committee, punctuate the serenity of ponds and swamps deep in the North Woods with their gentle "weeep weeep."

Whitetail deer at Peninsula State Park.

Male wood duck in breeding plummage.

Autumn north of the Tension Zone.

The North Woods mix of conifers and deciduous trees is most evident in autumn.

Winter in the pines.

These remarkable ducks take a leap of faith, one day after hatching—right out the entrance of their tree cavity nest, plummeting as much as six feet to the woodland floor below. After lining up behind Mom, this procession of downy fluffballs journeys to the nearest water and plunges in. Wood ducks are unique in the bird world in their degree of adaptation to both aquatic and woodland worlds. Their webbed feet, so functional in water, have sharp claws for grasping tree limbs. While most ducks' legs are placed relatively far back for water propulsion, wood ducks' legs are much farther forward—an asset when waddling into the forest for acorns. It's a pleasantly startling experience to be hiking deep in the woods and see this party-colored duck staring back from its perch on a tree limb.

At its peak, summer projects an aura of strength and permanence. But by late August, its solid green strength and bone-deep warmth are already beginning to fade. The green chlorophyll that has distinguished summer begins to loosen its grip as red tinges the leaves of a few maples.

As the autumnal equinox approaches in late September, fall is in full swing. Glowing red maples harmonize with yellow aspens and birches, with the translucent gold of tamaracks, with the purple ashes and the hard, mahogany-colored endurance of oaks. In adjacent wet meadows, fringed gentians raise their tubular blue bells to celebrate the season. The forest floor lights up with the mingled rusty golds of bracken ferns and the multiple reds and burgundies of unremembered shrubs. With each passing day, this sea of color ebbs and flows around the evergreens—defining, and being defined by, their deep green permanence.

Following this colorful zenith is a brief time of subtle enchantment. Leaves that once dominated the forest canopy now light up the forest floor; the woods are bright, open and airy, as a multitude of pastel hues are reflected on the slumbering tree trunks. And then it's over. All color fades and the woods sing in shades of gray, except for the quiet visual harmony of evergreens and white birches.

On their way south, Canada geese stop over at wetlands, to rest and gather strength. For a while these goose motels take on the air of an international airport, with geese constantly landing and taking off, gabbling and honking—as if disagreeing over flight plans and final destinations. And then they are gone. Loons and mergansers stay as long as they can, herding schools of fish into the shallows and feeding heavily; but ice finally closes in and pushes them south.

A brief time of quiet expectancy follows. And then snow flies in off the lake, covering the forest with its crystalline elegance. In this wintry blanket, snowshoe hare are concealed by their newly transformed white coats. Black bear bed down for their three-month winter sleep, and deer seek shelter from the cold and wind in cedar swamps. Against the backdrop of snow, white birches show their subtle colors. Soft pinks and warm tans glow faintly from deep inside the white bark. Birches and pines will carry the North Woods' visual spark of life through this time of simple elegance.

The antiquity of pines asserts itself as snow filters through their needles, and the wind sets these ancient instruments to singing. The massively calm chorus of millions of needles moves through the valleys and over the hills—whispering through our souls, connecting us with an ancient event that has repeated down through the ages. They invite us to join in their hymns of quiet joy, to celebrate being.

WETLANDS

At first glance, or first squishy step, wetlands are rather uninviting places. We often peer into swamps, bogs, and marshes from the edge because they require so much effort (and wet feet) to enter. Muck, water, and weeds—ick!—let's go to the beach! But wait; take another look; breathe deep the heady, spicy vapors. Here is one of the wildest, most alive, concentrated, and intimate ecosystems left.

Here is the modern-day version of life's original cradle. To the best of our knowledge, life began not in the depths of the ocean, or on the barren rocks; it was in the rich nutrient soup of the warm and shallow waters that amino acids first embarked on their cooperative ventures.

In a sense, we ourselves are self-contained, walking wetlands. Composed of over 57 percent water, our bodies are constantly moving water from one compartment to another and back again. Every one of our physiological processes is water dependent. And we still bear evidence of an earlier, wetter existence. In the first four weeks of embryonic life, developing humans exhibit gill arches and tails. Perhaps we are not as far removed from the wet wilds as we might like to think.

But what are wetlands? Definitions vary, but they all hover around a core description of lands saturated, or covered, with water for most, if not all, of the year. Wetlands are not just wet places; they are wet ecosystems where water depth is shallow enough for light penetration to stimulate characteristic wetland plants to thrive at all depths. The most commonly described types of wetlands are marshes, bogs, and swamps.

Marshes are nature's shallow cafeterias, nearly filled with cattails, rushes, and sedges in standing water up to three feet deep. Here spring is heralded by the territorial "kon-ke-reee" of red-winged blackbirds, and winter is foretold by muskrats' stepping-up repairs on their cattail lodges.

To enter a marsh is to enter one of the liveliest and most concentrated ecosystems on the planet—as productive as tropical rain forests, by some accounts. Plankton moves unseen in the water, as the air whirrs and buzzes with life. With each step, myriad life forms skitter and scatter over and through the water. A great blue heron's neck fires out and back again, triggered by a passing fish. Frogs hang suspended in a floating forest of duckweed. All manner of waterfowl benefit from the marsh. Bitterns stalk frogs and fish in the bulrushes, while ducks dabble and tip up, dining on submerged roots while their bobbing feet and bottoms put on a cartoon show above water.

But of all the plants and animals that thrive there, cattails and muskrats characterize the marsh better than any other pair. Cattails provide nesting material and food for many marsh rodents, but none make such effective use as muskrats. These furry little fake beavers give new meaning to the term "multiple use." They dine on cattail shoots in spring, munch the leaves and stems all summer long, and relish the

Sunrise in the marsh.

carbohydrate-rich roots throughout fall and winter. Muskrats are protected by a camouflage screen of cattails as they motor through the marsh. But they take this multiple use yet a step farther. They build lodges for shelter in much the same fashion as beaver, but for construction muskrats primarily use—you guessed it—cattails. And that's not all. In severe winters, when food supplies diminish, these frugal little rodents simply start nibbling on the walls of their edible wetland condos.

We often went to Lincoln Township Nature Center while finishing this chapter in December. This miniature wilderness remnant, within earshot of U.S. Interstate Highway 94, has a small marsh tucked behind Lake Michigan's dunes. Returning from the marsh one December morning, John wrote in his diary:

It was a bitterly cold and snowy day as I watched the vapor of muskrat breath rise from two small vent holes in the solitary lodge. In other times and places, I had listened to beaver kits mewing and whining deep inside their lodge, so I wondered what sounds a muskrat lodge might produce. Kneeling on the frozen marsh, snowflakes whirling all about, I leaned forward with my ear close to the lodge walls and heard . . . snoring.

The term "bog" is commonly misapplied to nearly any waterlogged terrain. In reality, a bog is a very specific and unique environment. Usually formed in steep-sided glacial depressions and virtually devoid of water movement, bogs are characterized by poorly oxygenated and acidic waters. The acidity and lack of oxygen are the prime limiting factors responsible for the unusual flora and limited fauna of bogs, as well as the bizarre nature of this floating world.

Bacterial decomposers are unable to flourish in this environment. Plant life, unable to survive in the depths of a bog's oxygen-starved water, grows first around the edges and then slowly over the surface. From the air, bogs have a bull's-eye appearance—with conifers (primarily spruce and tamarack) around the edges, and a mat of floating vegetation slowly closing in on the central eye of dark, tannin-stained water.

Composed of sphagnum moss, sedges, and evergreen heaths, the floating vegetation expands not only laterally, but also vertically. Unable to decompose, dead vegetation is pushed gradually downward as the living plants extend across the surface. This increasingly thick mat can often support a person's weight, but not without undulating like a vegetative wave. Sometimes spruces and tamaracks, having ventured out onto the thickest near-shore edge, quake along with the mat, their spires moving back and forth like ships' masts on a troubled sea. But tread lightly—bogs have a way of swallowing heavy-footed and careless

intruders, preserving them for discovery by some future paleobotanist intent on sifting through the buried pollen layers.

It's a tough life for a plant, making a living in a bog. Acid water, little oxygen, hardly any nitrogen from minimal biological decay—and all of this compounded by cold water that makes absorption of the minimal nutrients even more difficult. These same factors make life difficult for animals; limited wildlife may include shrews and voles, insects and spiders, treefrogs, garter snakes, and visiting birds.

But what bogs lack in biological diversity, they more than make up in imagination and adaptability. What engineer could have imagined and developed such brilliantly innovative designs as pitcher plants, sundews, and bladderworts? Each member of this carnivorous trio supplements its nitrogen- and mineral-poor diet by turning the tables on the animal kingdom.

Pitcher plants are the largest of the three, and most easily spotted by their funky green- and red-tinged hung-over flowers (one to a plant). At the base of the flower, a rosette of pitcher-shaped tubular evergreen leaves, partially filled with liquid, forms the business end of this plant. Insects are attracted by a sweet liquid secreted at the edge of the leaves. Downward-pointing hairs lining the inside of these tubes prevent insects from climbing out. As they take the easy route downward, insects become increasingly plastered with sticky platelets—and finally tumble into the enzyme-rich liquid to be digested into a nitrogen-rich bug soup, and absorbed.

The much smaller sundew has a similar physical arrangement, with a central flower and basal rosette of leaves. At the end of each leafstalk is a saucer-shaped leaf blade covered with hairs, each tipped with dewy, burgundy-colored glands. Attracted to these glistening glands, insects are stuck in super-glue fashion. The struggling insect seals its fate as movement triggers adjacent hairs, and finally the leaf blade itself, to fold over the insect. Within fifteen minutes, the hapless victim is dead; absorption of dissolved nutrients occurs over the next several days.

Bladderworts are a little more impatient. With their pretty little yellow flowers smiling smugly above the bog mat, bladderworts give little indication of the drama that goes on below. Not content to wait for small critters to wander into its traps, the bladderwort has evolved baglike traps on its underwater branches. These little bladders are primed when the water is sucked out by cells surrounding the cavity, creating a vacuum behind a one-way hinged door. When an unsuspecting mosquito larva brushes against trigger hairs, the hinged door flies open and the bladder expands, sucking in water and larva. The rest is familiar by now—bug soup.

A whitetail deer crosses a marsh at dawn.

A red-winged blackbird gives its territorial call from a cottonwood tree near the edge of a marsh.

Pitcher plants in the sphagnum mat of a bog (Wilderness State Park).

52

Marsh marigolds start the procession of spring wildflowers in the swamp.

Yellow lady's slippers bloom as white trilliums age to lavender.

As wetlands accumulate sediments and fill in from the accumulation of untold generations of plant life, woody-stemmed bushes and then trees begin to set up housekeeping. And it is trees that primarily distinguish swamps from other wetlands. It is also trees that are responsible for the miniature mountain-and-valley topography characteristic of swamps. Each wind-thrown tree that crashes to the ground creates a tip-up mound and trunk-length ridge. With time, and the creative gift of decomposition, the fallen tree is turned into rich humus. The tip-up mound and ridge become a nursery to a new generation of half a dozen or more trees. Here is tangible evidence of nature's recurring theme — the renewing cycle of creation out of dissolution, the transformation through death of old life to new.

At the base of each tip-up mound is a pool of water cradled in a depression once occupied by the uprooted tree. In the space of a few feet, the environment changes from aquatic to a soggy miniature shoreline, and up a decreasingly wet slope, to the comparatively dry tip-up mound peak. This concentrated assortment of microclimates produces a marvelous array of biological diversity.

Unique in any season, swamps put on their finest show in spring. This is a time of flowers, ferns, and fra-grance. In contrast to its heavy, pungent summer odor, the swamp now exudes a delicate, spicy earth smell. And the sudden yellow profusion of marsh marigolds flows through the swamp like a wave of adrenalin, jump-starting a profuse succession of wildflowers.

Here in this botanical meeting place is an uncommon assembly of early season wildflowers: violets and mitreworts, jack-in-the-pulpit, goldthread and starflower, spring beauty, trailing arbutus, bunchberry and bloodroot, to name but a few. As aging trilliums fade from bright white to soft lavender, yellow lady's slippers come of age in the damp slopes and depressions. When yellow lady's slippers begin to fade, moccasin flower is in its pink glory on the tip-up mounds. Showy lady's slippers complete the procession of these wild orchids, while cinnamon ferns have opened their fiddleheads. And the swamp plunges into the deep green of summer.

Marshes, bogs, and swamps — these are the main types of wetlands, but by no means all that there are. Swales and fens, ponds and wet sedge meadows — it's easy to get bogged down in wetland terminology.

And then there are coastal wetlands. These are wetlands of the types already described, but directly affected by Lake Michigan's capricious water-level

Coastal marsh in the Straits of Mackinac at Wilderness State Park.

This swale between ancient shorelines at the Ridges Sanctuary supports an abundance of life. The red blossom on the grown-over log belongs to a pitcher plant.

55

Situated at the northeast end of Lake Michigan, this succession of ancient shorelines exhibits a wooded dune and swale topography, interdunal wetlands, sand and gravel beaches, and a coastal marsh. This area provides refuge for more than two dozen rare and endangered species of plants and animals.

fluctuations. This is an important distinction. Unlike most wetlands that are ultimately filled in with biological growth and become meadows and forests, coastal wetlands do not exhibit this aging process. The flushing action of seiches, waves, and longer-term lake level fluctuations nearly eliminates permanent organic buildup. Alternating inundation and exposure keep any one type of growth from dominating, and these wetlands are continuously reborn.

A variety of wetlands can be found in lowlands all around Lake Michigan, tucked among dunes, in swales between ridges of ancient shorelines, and at the edge of rivers, streams, and lakes. Many state parks and forests feature wetlands, as do both national lakeshores and many nature centers and preserves.

It is important to understand that nicely packaged definitions are placed on dynamic natural systems. Definitions are created by and for human understanding. In reality, nature mixes swamps and marshes, and often flavors each with bits of bog. And all the while, the natural process is continuing to evolve new relationships and fine-tune ecosystems.

Since the first century A.D., when invading Romans attempted to drain the Fens of eastern England, people have waged an intense and persistent war against wetlands. This attitude spread, and eventually made landfall at Plymouth Rock with the Pilgrims; it traveled up the Erie and Welland canals with hopeful immigrants, and arrived with devastating consequences in the Lake Michigan Basin during the 1800s.

Where wetlands once cradled a phenomenal array of life, concrete jungles now squat on a squishy foundation of fill. Dunes at the south end of the lake were leveled and dumped into the wetlands. Chicago and Gary rose out of the swamps, marshes, and tamarack bogs, buoyed up on the displaced sands. This process was repeated all around the lake. Current estimates place the loss of wetlands in the Lake Michigan Basin at well over 50 percent of those present when Nicolet and his companions first paddled through the Straits of Mackinac in 1634.

So prevalent is the misconception of wetlands as dark, damp, and dangerous waste places that those of us finding beauty and life in them have often been made to feel guilty, perhaps even unbalanced. Unfortunately, many people have come to value all of nature in economic terms, as "resources." If the end use does not produce sufficient dollars, then we consider the resource to have inadequate value, and either waste, change, or destroy it—never mind the myriad life forms that depend on the devalued resource.

But attitudes and values are changing. We are beginning to see beyond the short-term dollar value of things. There is much more to assessing the worth of wetlands than computing their "development" potential. To find this true value requires consideration of their multiple and varied functions in the environment. When this is done, we arrive at a much more realistic value for these endangered life systems.

Environmental legislation of the 1970s and 1980s resulted in increased protection of wetlands, and in so doing created some strange bedfellows. Section 404 of the 1972 Clean Water Act placed the U.S. Army Corps of Engineers in charge of protecting wetlands from destruction by unrestricted filling and dredging. This was an event of considerable significance and irony. Previously, the Corps had been the government's sanctioned instrument for wholesale destruction of wet and soggy places.

In carrying out its new role, the Corps developed the following list of wetland functions and values:

1. *Natural biological functions*
   a. *net primary productivity*
   b. *food chain (web) support*
2. *Habitat for aquatic and wetland species*
3. *Aquatic study areas, sanctuaries and refuges*
4. *Hydrologic support functions*
   a. *shoreline protection from wave attack*
   b. *storage of storm and flood waters*
   c. *water purification through natural filtration, sediment trapping, and nutrient cycling uptake*
   d. *groundwater recharge*
5. *Cultural or auxiliary values including consumptive and nonconsumptive recreation as well as aesthetic value.*

For an agency that initially had trouble dealing with its new role as guardian of pollywogs and cattails, this was a remarkably accurate basic assessment of wetland functions.

Putting a dollar value on each of these functions, several studies have come up with economic assessments of the real value of wetlands. A 1986 study for the U.S. Fish and Wildlife Service listed the "economic value of Michigan's coastal wetlands" at over $2,000 per acre, per year. Other assessments have reported figures as high as $86,000 per acre. One study even found an increase in nearby residential property values based on proximity to wetlands.

Of special note are the hydrologic support functions. According to David Rains Wallace in *Life in the Balance,* several studies have shown that swamps store water with much less evaporation than do constructed reservoirs, that secondary sewage effluent is purified at a much lower cost than by treatment plants, and that stream flow is regulated much more economically by floodplain forests than by flood control reservoirs. At a time of deteriorating environmental quality, massive runaway budget deficits, a public near tax revolt, and aging water supply and treatment systems, the continued destruction of wetlands can only be viewed as self-destructive behavior.

We are finding that old perceptions of wetlands as expendable waste places are inadequate to the present, and dangerous to the future. What new insights and benefits, ecological and economic, might we discover in these still endangered environmental treasures?

Perhaps the greatest value of wetlands in this time of fractured ecosystems and increasing human alienation from the real and natural world is their ability to teach us about the diversity, adaptability, and interconnectedness of life in its many expressions.

ISLANDS

The cliffs, the shifting sands, the seagulls greet the sky;
Each living thing rejoices in this paradise.
And something in me yearns to be a part of life
In these islands.

— from the song "Islands," by Carol Johnson

We camped on a mountaintop in Lake Michigan recently. Consider that the wave-worn islands dotted throughout the lake's northern half are really the peaks of underwater mountains. From lonely islets barely more than a rock to archipelagoes full of variety, these small worlds are the summits of mountains reaching up from the deep. Completely surrounded by waters of an inland sea, they seem isolated and set apart; yet they share a connectedness, with both the encircling water and the submerged land mass.

Islands are different. They are places apart. From afar, these thin dark extensions of the horizon into the sky impart an air of mystery. At times they seem to hover above the water. Alternately seen and not seen, they appear and disappear in shrouds of mist. Islands stretch our imaginations, fostering a sense of curiosity and adventure.

These are the ingredients of myth and legend. Such qualities inspired early Native American beliefs in the sacredness of certain islands. The Manitous were revered isles, manifestations of the Great Spirit; even today, Garden Island holds the remains of an ancient hallowed Indian burial ground.

One of the best-known Indian legends is that of the mother bear and two cubs who swam across Lake Michigan to escape a Wisconsin forest fire. The exhausted cubs did not survive the long swim, but the faithful mother kept a steadfast vigil from shore. The

Great Manitou, touched by her devotion, raised the cubs above the water so she could see them again, creating the Manitou Islands; the mother's resting place became Sleeping Bear Dune.

Formation of two other islands was credited to the legendary hero Manabozho. Racing a wolf from the tip of the Leelanau Peninsula to Harbor Springs, he created a shortcut by tossing large chunks of earth and clumps of trees into Lake Michigan. Leaping across the stepping-stones, he won his race, and left the world the gifts of two new islands — North and South Fox.

Native American lore also tells of a young woman who lived along Lake Michigan's north shore, near Gros Cap. She was named Fringed Gentian, for her beauty was matched only by that of the delicate blue wildflowers that graced the nearby forests. When promised in marriage to an old but wealthy man, she was heartbroken. Unable to follow her father's wishes, she leapt off a tall cliff — into the arms of her true love. They paddled away to St. Helena Island, where they lived happily ever after. Wherever the radiant lovers strolled on the island, gentian seeds fell from her moccasins and grew in abundance. Even today, the beauty of fringed gentians adorns St. Helena Island.

Islands display some of the most magnificent beauty Lake Michigan has to offer — the coming together of sky and water, beach and forest. Many of the same natural features found on the mainland appear on

Ile aux Galets, a tiny island west of Cross Village, has just enough room for a lighthouse and a gull colony. Ridges can be seen extending underwater from this small mountaintop.

Viewed from North Manitou Island, South Manitou Island appears to hover on the horizon.

Islands are a concentrated interaction of land and sea.

islands: bogs, cedar swamps, meadows, sandy beaches, North Woods forests. Lake Michigan's northwestern chain of islands feature rocky shores and steep limestone cliffs, while the eastern isles support sweeping dunes and high bluffs. Common to all the islands is an abundance of shoreline. Where wave meets shore, there is the constant communication of both worlds; an island is isolated, yet always affected by the moving, changing water world.

Lake effect is strong here, where the waters mold both shore and weather. The cold, still wetness of fog envelops an island, until rays of sun burn through the mist, its diffuse goldness glowing as it rises. Sunlight sparkles on deep blue water and frothy white wave crests. Storm clouds tumble and roll across the sky, visible in their approach far across the expanse of sea; rainstorms beat on the water until air and land seem to approach the wetness of the lake itself. Island life is inescapably close to the natural processes. Even in an island's interior region, you are never far from the water, or its effects.

The water that gives an island its unique personality serves, at one time, as a barrier to accessibility, and at another time, as the very means of transportation to its shores. Humans reached islands long ago by fragile birchbark canoes. Today they come by modern ferries, private boats, and small planes. Islands were some of the first areas of European settlement on Lake Michigan. During early days of exploration and immigration, they were more accessible than roadless mainland regions—right on the watery highway, so to speak. Their harbors often gave shelter to ships in a storm, and their forests provided valuable firewood to fuel steamship engines. The variety of underwater structure provided an abundant harvest for fishing families whose lives were intricately linked with the water.

As the early water-based transportation system yielded to highways, railways, and airways, island life grew less accessible, less convenient, and more remote. Once bustling towns and busy farmlands now lie empty and still. But the lure has not died. Washington Island and Beaver Island, served by car ferries, each maintain a modest year-round population that swells seasonally with tourists and summer residents. Other smaller islands are havens for owners of private homes. Rock Island, North and South Manitou, and several of the Beaver Island group offer outstanding backpacking and camping experiences for those seeking solitude and a wilderness experience.

Part of an island's appeal is the journey required to reach it. This voyage allows time for reflection, an emotional letting go of all the things that claim us in our daily lives. Crossing an inland sea sparks a sense of adventure and requires a commitment of time. Voyagers take a risk, for transportation back to the mainland is dependent on ferry schedules and the whims of weather. Wind and waves may not allow passage. Island life demands flexibility.

This commitment required for an island journey creates a unique population—both tourists on a brief visit and permanent residents are islanders by choice. And the separation from the mainland can give a sense of freedom, for you cannot easily be called back. For a period of time, it is possible to know that rare experience of living in the present.

For many Lake Michigan islands, human visitation is occasional and fleeting. Permanent wildlife populations consist of only those species that have somehow managed to cross the water. Carried on wind or wave, these creatures arrive by flying, swimming, floating on driftwood and other debris, hitching a ride on boats, or crossing winter ice. While chance is usually a major factor in such voyages, certain species have been introduced to islands by people, such as the deer on both Beaver and North Manitou islands.

Animal populations vary greatly. Small, rocky islets may support only a few sandpipers, gulls, terns, toads, and insects—while Beaver Island, the largest in Lake Michigan, has a diversity approaching that of the mainland. Each island community is unique, a small world complete in itself. This isolation affects residents in unusual ways. When predators are absent, prey thrive and proliferate, creating abnormal concentrations, such as the abundant chipmunks on both North and South Manitou islands. Or, adapting to unusual living conditions, a species may develop peculiar characteristics. In a 1937 Cranbrook Institute of Science study of island animal life, Robert Hatt found toads on South Fox Island with a "condition of seeming gigantism." These large toads, averaging nearly four inches in length, walked rather than hopped, dragging their feet in six-and-a-quarter-inch strides and leaving trails up to four and a half inches wide.

While birds have much easier access to islands than other creatures, the diversity of species on islands is less than that of the mainland; the formidable expanse of water seems to limit even creatures gifted with flight. For some, however, remoteness is an advantage. Gulls, terns, cormorants, and others nest on the islands, at least partially isolated from human intruders and other predators. Bank swallows excavate tiny cave homes in steep sandy bluffs, while barn swallows take up residence in the vacant remains of weathered farm buildings. Great blue herons wade knee-deep through the wetlands, while loons cruise the waters of both inland island lakes and Lake Michigan.

During spring and fall migration, bird populations increase dramatically in numbers and diversity, as islands afford welcome rest areas from flight over open waters. Some of Lake Michigan's prime bird-

Terns at a High Island sandspit (Beaver Island archipelago).

Peninsula State Park on the Door Peninsula.

Orchards on Old Mission Peninsula benefit from the moderating lake effect of Grand Traverse Bay.

A chain of islands reaches from the Door Peninsula to the Garden Peninsula. Halfway across this chain lies St. Martin Island. Beyond are Poverty Island, Summer Islands, and the Garden Peninsula.

63

watching spots during migration are the islands—and their first cousins, the peninsulas. Birds following the shoreline as far as possible before crossing open water are often funneled to the tip of peninsulas.

Biologist William C. Scharf describes the migration of birds through the Leelanau Peninsula and offshore island chain as "a heavy concentration of brightly-colored birds: vireos, orioles, and warblers. Migrating with these small birds are a large number of hawks, which feed on the warblers—once described by a student as 'little salad birds.'" According to Dr. Scharf, it appears that migrating birds regularly make the six-mile crossing from Sleeping Bear Point on the Leelanau Peninsula to South Manitou Island's Lighthouse Point—"probably the premier migration spot in this area of the Great Lakes." From South Manitou's Gull Point, migrating birds continue "island-hopping" to North Manitou and beyond. Farther north, in the Beaver Island archipelago, High Island is the recipient of heavy migration in autumn; there, at certain times, Dr. Scharf has been able to band 150 birds before nine o'clock in the morning. Other sites of "tremendous migration" are Northport Point at the tip of the Leelanau Peninsula, and Waugoshance Point.

Dr. Scharf explains that there are three reasons why birds are drawn to islands and peninsulas during migration. First, when they migrate during the night and are caught over open water in the morning, "islands act as a magnet, as the birds are drawn to the first land they see." Second, because of the north-south alignment of these islands and peninsulas, the islands are natural "due-north extensions" of flight over the mainland peninsulas. Finally, Dr. Scharf theorizes that "birds simply *like* the islands. There seems to be something to this, for we have caught the same birds over and over on the same island, and these are banded birds that we know have traveled as far as South and Central America."

Bird migration pathways are only one of many similarities shared by islands and peninsulas. The name "peninsula" explains their likeness: from the Latin *paene* (almost) and *insula* (island), a peninsula is "almost an island"—surrounded by water on all sides but one. Like islands, peninsulas are blessed with an abundance of shoreline, and are profoundly affected by the lake that nearly encircles them. On these arms of land reaching far into the water, the lake effect creates prime growing conditions for orchards and vineyards—longer growing seasons and more moderate temperatures year-round. Because of their land connection, peninsulas are not so isolated as islands, but they too are out of the way. Travelers do not happen to pass through on the way elsewhere; they are there intentionally. This creates a smaller but perhaps more appreciative population, resident and visitor alike.

Peninsulas are geologically related to islands; a change in water level can create islands out of "almost islands," and vice versa. From the eastern shore, Waugoshance Point reaches toward the Beaver Island archipelago that, in ancestral Lake Chippewa, joined the mainland to form a much larger Waugoshance Peninsula. During that time of extremely low water, the Manitou islands may have been linked to the Leelanau Peninsula, and North Fox Island may have joined Waugoshance Peninsula—leaving a much larger South Fox as the only remaining island.

Today in the Green Bay area, two peninsulas are the bases of a chain of land features forming an arc of Niagaran dolomitic limestone that stretches across the lake. The Door and Garden peninsulas reach toward each other, with a series of islands guiding the way. Their gentle arches are mirrored throughout northern Lake Michigan—by Stonington Peninsula, Leelanau Peninsula, Old Mission Peninsula, and the chain of Manitou, Fox, and Beaver islands.

The wonderful mixture of shoreline features provided by these peninsulas and islands are irresistible: rugged limestone cliffs, expanses of beach, towering dunes, fjordlike harbors, bays sprinkled with islets, and island stepping-stones to the horizon. Sailors, tourists, campers, and residents alike are drawn by the scenic beauty—and by the chance to find peace and solitude. It seems that on a peninsula, the farther we travel toward the point, the farther we go into the past visually; remote areas, least touched by humans, impart views little changed over the ages.

Some of the most pristine areas of Lake Michigan exist on peninsulas, but the romance and mystique still belong to the islands—isolated little worlds with lives all their own, yet linked by the waters of which they are all a part. Within each microcosm small dramas go on daily, the seasons cycle, the lake exerts her unceasing influence, and life goes on—whether or not we are present. The islands at the north end of Lake Michigan appear as constellations in a night sea. Like those celestial worlds, they twinkle and beckon on the horizon, beacons calling us to a realm of beauty, magic, and mystery.

IN RETROSPECT

BEGINNINGS

In the early morning light, our canoe slid quietly through northern Lake Michigan's glassy water, as our spirits were buoyed by the rise and fall of gentle swells. For more than an hour, the dipping of our paddles blended into the rhythm of waves and swells, until we finally reached our destination — a cave in one of the sheer limestone cliffs, sculpted long ago by waves of ancestral Lake Nipissing.

A faint prehistoric rock painting marked the cave entrance, holding meanings unclear to us — but significant to Native Americans who long ago propelled flint-tipped projectiles into the rock shelter. Sitting in the same cave nearly 2,000 years later, we felt a sense of reverence for this ancient sacred place. Majestic stone pillars still supporting the open front of the cave added to the cathedral atmosphere. The same endless blue expanse of water stretched before us; waves lapped at the bright limestone shore below, and gulls soared and cried above. It was a timeless experience, surrounded by many of the same sights and sounds experienced so long ago by those Woodland Indians.

— Ann's diary, August 17, 1989

Standing knee-deep in Lake Michigan, toes wiggling as the surf arranges and rearranges the sand, we are directly connected not only with the present but also with the past and future. Always changing, the modern Great Lakes are Johnny-come-latelies in a long line of greater and lesser lakes. They were not the first, and odds are, they will not be the last inland freshwater seas in our northern Midwest.

Indian legend tells how the Creator gently supported Earth with his hand as he molded and shaped it. The outline of his hand is still evident in the shape of Michigan's Lower Peninsula. Modern people's understanding of the formation of this area is more scientific but no less fantastic, with great forces from deep within the earth, vast saltwater seas, and massive continental sheets of ice.

There was a time, a few billion years ago in the early Precambrian Era, when this region was alternately covered by volcanic islands, molten lava, and primordial seas. At this time, humans were not even a conceptual glimmer on the evolutionary horizon— neither was Lake Michigan. Subterranean instabilities resulted in the creation of entire mountain ranges, that were subsequently eroded to small hills and mildly contoured plains by that most yielding and yet most powerful of substances, water. Several such mountain-building episodes, known among geologists as orogenies, came and went.

As the Precambrian Era closed, approximately 500 to 600 million years ago, the near constant state of flux and upheaval of the earth's crust in the Great Lakes area subsided. The following Paleozoic Era was a time of comparative calm and geologic stability; it was also a time of shallow saltwater seas that ebbed and flowed across as much as two-thirds of what is now North America. With the draining off or drying up of each sea, significant layers of sediment remained. Some of these sediments are of considerable economic impor-

An ancient sea cave in a dolomitic limestone cliff at the north end of Lake Michigan is believed to have been used by Middle Woodland Indians for religious ceremonies.

tance today — yielding oil and natural gas, gypsum, limestone, and rock salt.

A sinking trend centered in Michigan's Lower Peninsula created the Michigan structural basin, which accumulated as much as 14,000 feet of layered sediment during the alternating flooding and drying up of Paleozoic seas. These slightly tilted sedimentary rock layers responded in different ways to subsequent erosional forces, creating major topographic features that would eventually help determine the location and margins of modern Lake Michigan. Shales and other weak rock layers were more easily removed, in areas near the edges of the Michigan Basin that would later be filled by the waters of Lakes Michigan and Huron. More erosion-resistant rock formed an arc that would one day rim the northern shores of these same two Great Lakes. Thus, Lake Michigan was conceived. Not born, mind you, conceived; the actual birth awaited the coming of the glacial midwives.

A very erosion-resistant form of limestone called dolomite was formed in the seas of the Silurian Period of the Paleozoic Era, with the addition of magnesium to the calcium carbonate of limestone in the marine environment. This process continued for millions of years along the northern edges of the Silurian Seas. What may seem a ho-hum event brought about a not so ho-hum result — the relatively tough, erosion-resistant escarpments that rock and roll along the cliffs and islands of the north shores of Lakes Michigan and Huron, as well as parts of other Great Lakes. One of these dolomitic escarpments, the Niagaran, surfaces to form the Garden and Door peninsulas in northern Lake Michigan, the Bruce Peninsula and Drummond and Manitoulin islands in Lake Huron, and Niagara Falls between Lakes Erie and Ontario. As honeymooner and hiker, tourist and sightseer stand at these sites feeling an intangible connectedness with the natural processes, their feet feel a direct connection — via dolomitic limestone — to the Paleozoic Era and all the little lime-secreting marine organisms that helped create these magnificent views.

Not to be outdone by the Silurian Period, the Devonian Period of the Paleozoic Era produced leftovers that, to countless thousands of bent-over children and adults, are a treasured creation of prehistoric times — the Petoskey stone. These fossilized fragments of the colonial coral *Hexagonaria,* with their symmetrical designs, were once part of coral reefs growing in warm shallow Devonian seas at the edge of the Michigan Basin. Today these little time capsules are most commonly found along the beaches of Little Traverse Bay near Petoskey, Michigan. They have also been found as far south as Sleeping Bear Dunes, and inland in northern lower Michigan, along lake shores and in excavations.

Although not a time of marked geologic activity, the first half of the Paleozoic Era was a time when life — plant and animal — virtually exploded in numbers and types. Algae and corals filled the shallows, and brachiopods waved their gills in hopes of directing a passing morsel into their mouths; trilobites cruised the bottoms, and prehistoric sharks cruised wherever they pleased. Except for mammals and birds, animals representing every phylum and class appeared during this era. During the latter half of the Paleozoic Era, from approximately 345 million to 230 million years ago, things changed. In the Lake Michigan area, the earth's crust underwent foldings and upliftings, and the seas receded, leaving broad valleys and rivers — a roadway for icy events yet to come.

The rocks and fossils of the Precambrian and Paleozoic eras have spoken with clarity, providing us with a remarkable amount of knowledge about these times. However, with the close of the Paleozoic Era, the rocks go nearly silent. With the exception of a few Late Jurassic red beds located underneath glacial drift, there are no rocks younger than 280 million years old in the Lake Michigan area. Geologists have named this 280-million-year gap in the record the Lost Interval.

In other areas of the world, the Lost Interval was a time of considerable geological, botanical, and biological activity. First mammals appeared, followed by birds, flowering plants, primates, and grasses. As recently as one to two million years ago, the first humans came loping over the evolutionary horizon. How much of this activity took place in the Great Lakes area is purely speculation.

The rocks and fossils that could have spoken to us were partly removed by erosion; but it was not until the extensive destruction by the Pleistocene glaciers that the majority of evidence was obliterated. As the glaciers came rumbling down the valleys and oozing over highlands, they scoured and ground the more recent rocks, plants, and slow-moving animals of the Mesozoic and Cenozoic eras right down to the late Paleozoic — scattering their pulverized and mostly illegible remains all over the countryside.

Approximately 2 million years ago, the Pleistocene Ice Age was ushered in by a cooling of the earth's temperature and a gradual buildup of snow in the arctic and subarctic regions. As these snows continued to accumulate, they went through a metamorphosis to glacial ice. When the glacier reached a critical mass, its own tremendous weight caused it to begin to move and flow outward at the edges. There were four glaciations interspersed by interstadials, warmer interludes that temporarily melted the glaciers back to their northern birthing grounds. Nearly all topographic evidence of the first three glaciations has been obliterated by the last glaciation, called the Wisconsinan — the

Still marking the entrance to the cave is a rock painting, thought to symbolize a sweat lodge rite. In this ritual, a large "messenger stone" was heated by fire, then sprinkled with water. Purifying steam rose, carrying messages to the Indians' Manitou (Spirit).

Erosion-resistant limestone cliffs of the Niagaran Escarpment are pounded and carved by Lake Michigan's waves at Cave Point in Door County.

one responsible for the modern Great Lakes.

These glaciers were absolutely mind-boggling in size and power. Picture, for a moment, a sheet of ice over two miles thick at the center and over a quarter mile thick at the active front—a sheet of ice covering over 10 million square miles, stretching across the width of the North American continent with its southerly edge extending as far as southern Indiana. The Wisconsinan glacier was somewhat smaller—over one million square miles in area; its southern margin extended to central Indiana and Illinois.

Contemplating the size of these glaciers weighs heavily on the imagination; the glacier itself weighed heavily on the earth's crust, depressing it by as much as 3,000 feet to the north in Hudson Bay. This is significant, not only in its WOW! potential, but also because what goes down must come up, geologically speaking. As the last advance of the Wisconsinan Glacier receded, the earth's crust began to rebound slowly, and continues to do so north of the hinge line connecting Kewaunee, Wisconsin to Manistee, Michigan.

This last glaciation followed the path of its older siblings through an ancient rocky road formed by the river valleys and erosion-resistant escarpments of earlier times. As the glacier moved over the land, it ground and pulverized softer limestones and shales to

sand and "rock flour." What it didn't pulverize, it picked up and stored in its icy bulk until it began to melt and recede, dropping these boulders as glacial erratics in distant lands.

The glacier shaped the landscape not only by what it removed, but also by what it left behind. Moraines—large ridges of unsorted boulders, gravel, sand, and clay—were left at the glacier's edge. The moraines that rise as high as two hundred feet above lake level to ring the southern end of Lake Michigan mimic the glacial lobe that sat melting there 14,000 years ago. As the ice receded, its meltwaters were dammed up behind these moraines (as they are today), and a series of proglacial lakes were formed, the first being named Lake Chicago.

It took over 3,000 years from the time the glacier packed up and left the area that is now the south end of Lake Michigan until it finally bid adieu to the north end. As thousands of years passed, drainage outlets continued to change. Lakes rose and fell, creating a complex and not entirely understood ancestral lake sequence—the study of which has caused much snoring in libraries throughout the land.

One of Lake Michigan's predecessors is, nonetheless, of interest to those enamored with the wilds of current Lake Michigan. Lake Nipissing, the next to last of Lake Michigan's ancestors, was also one of the largest and highest. For over 1,000 years, Lake Nipissing's wave actions shaped shoreline features that endure today, including wave-cut cliffs, sea caves, and terraces. Lake Nipissing is responsible for the abandoned beach ridges of Wisconsin's Point Beach State Forest and the Ridges Sanctuary at Baileys Harbor, as well as many embayment lakes, such as Michigan's Crystal, Hamlin, Torch, and Elk lakes. Perhaps most dramatic of all Lake Nipissing's gifts are the towering sand dunes rimming much of Lake Michigan's eastern shores.

For the last 2,000 to 3,000 years, the Great Lakes have remained relatively stable. This is a temporary stability, for even the inland seas of the Great Lakes are, on a geologic time scale, fleeting and fragile entities. Further crustal rebound and erosion of outlets will no doubt continue to alter the shape and depth of Lake Michigan. Over time, deposition of sediments from run-off and the settling of plant and animal debris will cause a filling in of shallow parts of the lake, eventually resulting in large and fertile plains.

However, the existence of Lake Michigan in some future form is not necessarily doomed. The wanderlust of the continental glaciers may not be over. In 1976, Hays, Imbrie, and Shackleton published the results of their study of orbital, geologic, and radioactive data, indicating a periodic repetition of the factors that cause ice ages. Their theory, accepted by many geologists and climatologists, suggests that the earth is past the midpoint between the last glaciation and the next.

It appears likely that, in several thousand years, ice now slumbering in the polar regions will wake up, pack its bags, and head south for the winter. Once again a glacier may travel the ancient rocky road, bulldozing and pulverizing the softer materials in its path, depressing the earth's crust, leaving terminal and recessional moraines, and damming up meltwaters—birthing new inland freshwater seas to be explored by new generations.

The great glaciers of the Ice Age have profoundly affected human existence, from the dramatic changes in climate and environment during glaciation to the geologic features left by their retreat. In fact, the glaciers probably made possible the first human immigration to the North American continent. It is believed that the huge continental ice mass drew off enough of the earth's surface water to dramatically lower ocean levels, linking Asia to North America by a temporary land bridge.

Who knows what stimulated those prehistoric peoples to pack up and head east into a new and mysterious land: wars, hunger, or that most basic of human drives, curiosity? Whatever the cause, these brave Asian souls advanced onto the North American continent and continued eventually into the primordial Lake Michigan area. These ancient explorers were the true "discoverers" of the Great Lakes area—nearly 13,000 years before French explorers arrived in the 1600s.

Standing on the shore of the early postglacial lake, these people must have enjoyed a view that would seem strange to us today. There lay the beautiful blue expanse of water—but far on the horizon loomed a great wall of ice, in its slow retreat. Near this icy wall, the most recently exposed land sprouted tundra and wetlands. As vegetation spread northward on the heels of the glacier, spruce-fir forests gradually followed. These thick forests crowded out most understory vegetation, providing inadequate food for most animals (and humans); thus, early nomadic hunters found the most plentiful game in the wetlands, tundra, and tundra-forest transition zone. And so they followed the glacier in its northward retreat.

What fascinating wildlife they hunted! In addition to deer, elk, and caribou, there were piglike peccaries, woodland musk oxen, giant mooselike *Cervalces,* hairy elephants (mammoths and mastodons), and even giant beavers. These beavers were comparable in size to modern black bears—eight to nine feet in length, weighing as much as 480 pounds! Archaeological finds also suggest that whales and walruses once cruised and lounged around the postglacial lakes, including Lake Chicago in the Lake Michigan Basin.

These creatures were witnesses to, and sometimes victims of, tremendous environmental changes over the millennia of glacial retreat. Postglacial lakes formed, and water levels rose or fell—depending on the changing routes of drainage. At one time in the Lake Michigan Basin, Lake Chicago (11,000 B.C. to 10,000 B.C.) was as much as sixty feet higher than the present water level. By 7500 B.C., water levels of ancestral Lake Chippewa had dropped to 350 feet below present levels.

As early Lake Michigan was forming, changing, evolving, so were its inhabitants. The earliest known Native Americans in the Lake Michigan area were nomadic hunters who used spears with points of chipped stone. These carefully crafted points were fluted, or grooved longitudinally, for attachment to the split shaft of a spear. It is believed that these Paleo-Indians hunted large game—caribou, musk oxen, even mammoths and mastodons.

These earliest humans were the first in a series of prehistoric Native American cultures inhabiting the Lake Michigan Basin from about 11,000 B.C. to 1600 A.D. Over centuries, cultural patterns appeared and flourished, then disappeared as groups migrated, were wiped out (by famine, epidemics, or war), or shifted traditions to new cultural patterns (adapting to changing environment, or as a result of contact with other cultures). In addition to hunting, subsistence depended on fishing, trapping, gathering (seeds, nuts, berries, and roots), and eventually agriculture. Ancient stone and woodworking tools were developed. Improved weapons included the spear-thrower, for propelling a spear with increased force. As early as 7,000 B.C., boats were gliding across Lake Michigan's ancestral waters.

By 5000 B.C., Native Americans of the Old Copper Culture were crafting tools, weapons, and ornaments from copper. Initially, the copper was a "gift" of the glaciers, carried from the Lake Superior Basin and left in glacial drift as the ice receded. Later, these prehistoric Native Americans also mined copper from surface outcrops on Lake Superior's Keweenaw Peninsula and Isle Royale. Archaeology authority George Quimby describes them as "the first fabricators of metal in the Americas and perhaps in the whole world." From pure copper they formed various implements "by coldhammering and annealing—pounding the copper and heating and chilling it to keep it from becoming too brittle"—remarkably advanced for a people often perceived as primitive!

In the Lake Michigan area, the Copper Culture mostly occupied the northern shores. It was a different and radically changing environment inhabited by these people. As the glacial retreat cleared the Straits of Mackinac, drainage outlets opened to the east, and water levels dropped hundreds of feet in ancestral Lake Chippewa.

During this low-water stage of Lake Michigan, a long river flowed through a steep canyon at the Straits of Mackinac to Lake Huron's predecessor, Lake Stanley. This ancient riverbed now lies deep underwater, between the towers of the Mackinac Bridge. On Lake Chippewa's northern shores, rivers tumbled and fell two to three hundred feet over limestone hills, in great rapids and waterfalls. The Garden Peninsula's Burnt Bluff was a steep inland mesa. The Beaver Island archipelago was joined to the mainland, creating a large peninsula. Green Bay was a lowland valley. The present-day Chicago area was thirty miles from the lake, and as much as 370 feet above water level. But the water eventually rose again, leaving many prehistoric habitation sites as much as 300 feet under water. (This puts our current-day concerns over changing lake levels in a different perspective.)

Changes in climate and water levels continued. As the climate warmed and hardwoods and grasslands moved northward, plant foods became increasingly available. While hunting and fishing remained essential, dependence on gardening and agriculture gradually increased—especially south of the Tension Zone. Archaeologists refer to this cultural period beginning around 1000 B.C. as the Woodland Period. Characteristics of these cultures included plant cultivation, pottery making, and mound building.

Many Native Americans of the Woodland Period participated in an extraordinary trade network that reached far across the country. Ornate crafts used obsidian and grizzly bear teeth from the Rocky Mountains, pearls and sea shells from the south Atlantic coast and the Gulf of Mexico, mica sheets (for mirrors) from the mid-Atlantic coast, copper and silver from western Lake Superior, lead from Missouri and northwestern Illinois.

The people of the Hopewell tradition, a major development in Woodland cultures, also constructed elaborate mounds. One of several uses of these mounds was burial, with art objects, tools, and weapons placed in the mounds with the bodies. The largest known Hopewell ceremonial center in the Lake Michigan Basin was at the present location of Grand Rapids: two groups of mounds totaling more than forty-five—the largest with a height of thirty feet and circumference of two hundred feet.

As traditions and cultural patterns changed, Hopewell customs disappeared about 700 A.D. From that time until about 1300, an Effigy Mound culture created unique mounds in shapes resembling animals and birds. Not all were burial mounds; in those that were, the deceased were buried at the head or heart of the creature. These unusual mounds have been identified primarily in Wisconsin. Few of the estimated 5,000 original mounds remain today; however, two parks in the Lake Michigan area exhibit good examples. Indian Mound Park at Sheboygan, Wisconsin, features sixteen mounds, including deer and panther. At Lizard Mound Park near West Bend, Wisconsin, twenty-eight mounds include panther, bird, and lizard effigies. In the preindustrial absence of front-end loaders, or even modern shovels, the construction of these mounds required a remarkable effort. At Lizard Mound Park, the lizard is over 250 feet long, and a bird effigy is over 300 feet in length.

A number of different native cultures occupied the Lake Michigan region from 800 A.D. to 1600 A.D., referred to as the Late Woodland Period. Descendants of these tribes were present when the first white explorers appeared on the scene. The Great Lakes tribes of that time came from three basic stocks, or major linguistic groups: Iroquoian, Algonquian, and Siouan. On Lake Michigan in the early 1600s, Winnebagos in the Door County/Green Bay region, and Dakotas southwest of Green Bay were of Siouan stock. Hurons, of Iroquoian stock, lived primarily in the Lake Huron region; however, later driven by Iroquois war parties, they intermittently occupied Michilimackinac and Potawatomi Island (believed to be Door County's

Fossils found on the Lake Michigan shore are remains of inhabitants of Paleozoic saltwater seas, such as corals (including Petoskey stones), crinoids, and trilobites.

A young traveler contemplates a much older traveler—a glacial erratic boulder carried and deposited by Pleistocene glaciers.

72

Sleeping Bear Plateau rises 450 feet above Lake Michigan. The perched dune itself is a relatively thin layer of sand atop the sediments of a glacial moraine.

Panther effigy mound at Lizard Mound Park.

Rock Island). Most of the tribes around Lake Michigan belonged to the Algonquian stock. Around 1600, Ojibway occupied the northern shores. Menomini, Sauk, and Fox inhabited the Green Bay region, while Miami lived along the southern third of the lake. On the eastern side, Potawatomi and Ottawa occupied Michigan's lower peninsula. The coming of Europeans was to thoroughly disrupt these population patterns, and an entire way of life.

The Native Americans' adaptation to life in the wilderness was remarkable; they skillfully and efficiently used what raw materials nature provided. Today's romantic notion of "living off the land" was a fact of life for these people. They harvested wild rice, gathered edible plants and berries, and tapped sugar maples in springtime. Fishing yielded abundant catches of whitefish and sturgeon. In the warmer southern regions, they developed agricultural skills, relying primarily on corn, beans, and squash.

Hunting and trapping was vital to subsistence, especially in the northern regions where a short growing season discouraged agriculture. A wide variety of game was taken with bows and arrows, spears, snares, and traps. These creatures provided not only nourishment, but also skins and furs for blankets, moccasins,

and clothing — and bones for tools, utensils, fish hooks, and artistically carved ornaments.

The earth was a provider: stones and flint for weapons and tools, and clay to produce pottery and ornaments. Wood was carved into bowls and utensils. Rushes and reeds were woven into baskets, mats for sitting and sleeping, and larger panels to cover a sapling framework for shelter. Shelters were also covered with skins or bark.

Birch bark (or elm where birch was unavailable) was skillfully crafted into buckets and storage containers, and one of the best-known and most remarkable "primitive" inventions — the canoe. This lightweight, well-designed craft could carry amazing loads on long voyages down rivers and across open waters of inland seas, yet was easily carried overland on portages. To this day, the canoe remains one of the most efficient and seaworthy small crafts in use.

As R. Clyde Ford has written, "Indians knew the way of the wild creatures as the white men could never know. They were Nature's children and schooled in the lore of the wilderness." These skills that allowed Native Americans to live a life so closely related to the land were not just accidental discoveries, but intelli-

Burial ground on Garden Island, used by Native Americans from prehistoric to recent times (Beaver Island archipelago).

74

A dolomite boulder on the north shore catches the last warm rays of daylight.

gently crafted abilities passed from generation to generation. Along with these skills were passed a system of religious beliefs that also reflected a life intertwined with the natural world.

Each tribe had individual beliefs; however, most shared a belief in a single Creator. They saw all things as having a spiritual essence. Viewing themselves as one part of this Creation, they saw a familial relationship with their environment — referring to "father" sun and "mother" earth. Legends and mythology helped explain the world about them, performing the same function as the white people's religious legends and myths. Ceremonies, songs, prayers, and offerings perpetuated a close relationship with the Creator, everything in nature, and the cycles of life. Personal "manitos," or guardian spirits, were found through fasting and dreaming.

Native Americans saw life in all things — life that deserved respect. These people whose lives depended on their environment understood the importance of treating nature with reverence. They took what they needed and used it efficiently, avoiding waste and abuse of their natural world. Their communion with the creatures and forces of nature, and their view of all beings as family was, and is, significant. They understood better than today's "enlightened" culture how closely interrelated all of life really is.

When white explorers first "discovered" the Great Lakes, they found a well-established, though quite different, culture — people who had made an intelligent and resourceful adaptation to life in the natural world. Tribes were socially and politically organized, usually quite democratically; leaders were chosen by consent of all members, and served as representatives and spokesmen, rather than rulers. Intertribal alliances and confederacies existed throughout the area, usually within the same linguistic stock. Trade networks reached across much of the country, with a system of trails whose routes are still followed today by modern highways. But this period of relative stability was nearing its end, as the Great Lakes waterways were carrying new, paler, bearded faces — with new ideas, agendas, and perspectives.

THE WHITE WAVE

America would not be in the mess it is today if the Indian had had stricter immigration laws.
— Chief Oshkosh

From the earliest European explorations, the history of Lake Michigan has been one of surprise and discovery. This freshwater sea is not what was expected. In 1634, Jean Nicolet, one of Champlain's young explorers, paddled west from the Straits of Mackinac, fully expecting to greet the citizens of Cathay (China) on the other side. Nicolet was the latest in a series of determined explorers in quest of the western route to the exotic riches of China, also known as the Indies. He had been preceded in the New World by Vikings, Columbus, Cabot, Verrazano, Cartier, Champlain, and Brule. Nicolet was lured to Lake Michigan by natives' stories of great seas beyond the St. Lawrence River where a tribe called "People of the Sea" lived on the western shore.

We can only guess Nicolet's thoughts and feelings as he and his companions pulled their paddles through the pristine waters of northern Lake Michigan. But one thing was certain—he came prepared, for he had heard of the beautifully decorated and fine robes worn by the citizens of Cathay. As they neared the shores of Green Bay on the Door Peninsula, he donned a fantastic damask robe decorated with birds and flowers— this over buckskins, and most likely with an unshaven and not-so-clean explorer's face. He stepped on shore, raising and ceremoniously firing two pistols. When the smoke cleared, so the story goes, he was amazed and disappointed to be greeted not by Chinese, but by equally amazed Winnebago Indians.

Had they realized Nicolet was the advance guard for the explorers, fur traders, settlers, tourists, trucks, and recreational vehicles that would someday overrun their land, the Winnebagos probably would have sent Nicolet packing. As it was, they greeted him with considerably more courtesy and acceptance than was shown to Indians by the white wave to come. Once again, a portion of the New World—already peopled by a civilized and friendly race—was "discovered" by another intrepid European explorer.

The 1600s was a watershed time in Great Lakes human history. After millennia of gradual change and development in both the environment and its inhabitants, both were on the brink of sudden and dramatic upheaval. The collision of two very different cultures brought benefits and losses. The benefits weighed heavily on the European side. For these newcomers, there was a new world—full of promise and opportunity. Native Americans served as their guides in exploration and their allies in wars. They shared with the whites their knowledge, including the use of canoes and snowshoes, and other ways of survival. Europeans saw in the Great Lakes a seemingly endless supply of natural resources: furs and pelts for high fashion, land to be cleared for agriculture, timber for building homesteads and eventually cities.

For the Native Americans (who were given the misnomer "Indian" by Europeans), benefits were few and losses enormous. They welcomed the goods brought by early traders—brass kettles, iron hatchets and other tools, jewelry and beads, textiles, and guns—all which seemed an improvement on the traditional products they replaced. But traders also brought alcohol and encouraged its use; Indians were totally unprepared to deal with the resulting demoralizing drunkenness, aggressiveness, and addiction. Europeans also unknowingly brought new deadly diseases to

During the reenactment of a voyageurs' rendezvous, a voyageur canoe replica arrives at the Straits of Mackinac.

the natives—smallpox, diphtheria, scarlet fever, measles, and tuberculosis. With no natural immunity, the death rates in affected villages reached 70 to 80 percent, as epidemics ravaged tribes throughout the area.

Early Great Lakes explorers were repeatedly frustrated in their quest for a route to the Orient, but Europe quickly recognized a far different wealth in this wilderness—animal furs. In particular, beaver pelts were highly prized by European fashion trend-setters, and the supply of beaver in this vast watery wilderness seemed endless. In return for beaver pelts and other furs, natives welcomed the trade goods offered them. And so the Indians were catapulted from a late Stone Age existence into the center of a worldwide industry and trade network.

The search for trade routes to China was a dream that died hard and continued to inspire some explorers. But an intensifying drive for expansion of the fur trade and international competition for control of this rich new land spurred on New World explorations. Lake Michigan was a key link in the exploration routes that followed Nicolet's journey.

In 1673, Father Jacques Marquette and French-Canadian explorer Louis Joliet embarked from the Straits, lured by Indian tales of a mysterious river called *Mississippi* (Great River) that flowed south to the sea. They paddled Lake Michigan's shoreline to Green Bay's Fox River, which eventually led them to the Mississippi River. Returning through the Chicago Portage (Illinois and Des Plaines Rivers), they followed Lake Michigan's western and northern shores back to the Straits. These were two of the three main routes to the Mississippi River later followed by Jesuit missionaries, explorers, fur-trading voyageurs, and settlers.

The third major route to the Mississippi was first used by René Robert Cavelier, Sieur de La Salle, whose dreams were as big as his name. He envisioned establishing a French fur trading empire on the Great Lakes and the Mississippi, using cargo-carrying sailing ships. The *Griffon*, built above that great obstacle to shipping, Niagara Falls, became the first ship to sail the Great Lakes in August of 1679. But it soon earned a more infamous place in history as the first Great Lakes shipwreck. Loaded with furs and headed for Niagara, the *Griffon* set sail from Potawatomi Island (most likely Door County's Rock Island) on September 18, 1679—never to be seen again. Whether victim of a sudden storm or other unknown tragedy, the *Griffon* became Lake Michigan's first recorded unsolved maritime mystery.

Unaware of his ship's ill fate, La Salle and his men made an arduous canoe trip along the western and southern shores of the lake to the mouth of the Miami (St. Joseph) River; there they erected a stockaded fort while awaiting the expected return of the *Griffon,* with fresh supplies. When the ship did not arrive, La Salle continued on by way of the St. Joseph and Kankakee rivers—the third major route linking Lake Michigan and the Mississippi River. The loss of the *Griffon* was the first of many setbacks to La Salle's plans, but he did eventually win his claim to fame as the first European explorer to reach the mouth of the Mississippi River at the Gulf of Mexico.

Along with explorers and traders, the European fur trade brought to the Lakes region Jesuit missionaries, soldiers, and tumultuous times in the 1600s. Even before the French were living and trading directly with natives on Lake Michigan, the fur trade had already begun to disrupt lifestyle and population patterns. To the east, the Dutch and British wanted a piece of the action, and set up trade with Iroquois Indians. The Iroquois operated as intermediaries between other Indian tribes and Europeans, as did the Hurons. These Indians were swept into the wave of fur-trading competition, and long-smoldering intertribal conflicts erupted into wars for control of beaver territories.

Well-armed with weapons from their white allies, Iroquois invaded and devastated the Huron territory. Huron survivors fled westward. Many other tribes soon followed—refugees of the nearly complete depopulation of Michigan's lower peninsula by Iroquois war parties. By 1672, Wisconsin's Fox River Valley was teeming with refugees; so concentrated was this group of people that many died of starvation that winter. Truces held only temporarily; it was not until after 1700 that attacks on the French and their Indian allies waned.

As the fur empire grew, colorful French voyageurs arrived on Lake Michigan, singing lustily as they paddled thirty-five- to forty-foot birchbark canoes that held up to twelve men and 6,000 pounds of cargo. These "Montreal canoes" arrived loaded with trade goods for Indians, and departed piled high with bundles of furs. Moving inland from the big lake, voyageurs used smaller "north canoes"—twenty-five feet long, holding up to 3,000 pounds—to maneuver the rivers and streams, and to carry across the long portages. Fur trading centers on Lake Michigan grew at key locations: Michilimackinac, Green Bay, Milwaukee, Chicago, and Fort St. Joseph on the St. Joseph River.

The effects of this seemingly simple fur-trading industry were far-reaching. It motivated exploration, stimulated early settlement, restructured the lifestyle of an entire native people, and was the direct cause of more than one international war. This ongoing struggle for control of beaver country entangled the French, British, Dutch, Spanish, and eventually the Americans in conflict; Indians were often drawn into the rivalry,

For much of the 18th century, the fortified community of Fort Michilimackinac (now restored) was a center of the fur trade and an important post during military struggle for control of the region.

The traditions of its original Dutch settlers are still celebrated in Holland, Michigan.

contending with shifting alliances.

By 1763, at the close of the French and Indian War, France relinquished all its North American claims to the victorious British. But that same year, Indian grievances against the new British authorities erupted into open rebellion. Attacks on many Great Lakes forts were inspired by Ottawa Chief Pontiac. On Lake Michigan, Fort St. Joseph fell, and two-thirds of the British soldiers at Fort Michilimackinac were killed in surprise attacks.

With France out of the picture, the prime contenders for control of Lake Michigan were the British and their rebellious American colonists (with the exception of a brief seizure of Fort St. Joseph by the Spanish in 1781). Even after the end of the American Revolution in 1783, the British refused to leave the Great Lakes area and relinquish control of their holdings. This was one of the prime causes of the War of 1812, after which the British-American borders were firmly established.

By the 1830s and 1840s, the supply of fur-bearing animals was finally dwindling, as was the fur trade. After nearly two centuries of adapting their lives to this fur trade, Native American tribal structure and culture had broken down. Now dependent on European goods, they had no money (furs) with which to purchase them. Impoverished of both money and their old adaptive skills, Indians were in an ideal position to be taken advantage of. The wave of settlers from the east had begun, and the newcomers wanted land.

Beginning in the late 1700s and continuing into the 1800s, a long series of Indian treaties and land cessions took place. In exchange for their land, Native Americans received cash, annual payments, and a variety of trade goods and supplies. During such treaty negotiations, the plentiful supply of alcohol made available to the Indians decreased their resistance to unacceptable terms. At the same time, traders were encouraging Indians to go into debt, which in turn stimulated further land sales. Often, treaty negotiators dealt with one select chief who would sign without resistance, but who did not represent the tribe's wishes.

Native Americans did not believe in land ownership, but believed the land was a gift from the Great Spirit, to be taken care of. In the words of one North American Indian leader: "We shall consider your offer to buy our land. What is it that the White Man wants to buy, my people will ask. It is difficult for us to understand. How can one buy or sell the air, the warmth of the land? That is difficult for us to imagine. If we don't own the sweet air and the bubbling water, how can you buy it from us?" With a long heritage based on the concepts of communal ownership, cooperation, and sharing, Native Americans initially believed they were agreeing to *share* the land with the new white neighbors.

In the early 1830s, white Americans saw two basic solutions to the "Indian problem": "civilization" (remolding Indians in the image of the whites), or removal of all Indians to a large reservation on the open prairies west of the Mississippi River. When "civilization" proved ineffective, Congress passed the Indian Removal Act in 1830. In treaties of 1833 and 1836, under growing official pressure and threat of removal, Native Americans signed over to the United States nearly all remaining holdings around Lake Michigan.

In 1840, General Hugh Brady sent troops and agents to carry out the final removal of Indians from Michigan and Indiana. Many natives fled to Canada; others successfully hid in remote areas. But over a thousand were rounded up and forced to march west. In the St. Joseph River valley, the Potawatomi leader Leopold Pokagon shrewdly used the law to prevent removal of his people. With funds from previous land cession treaties, they had previously purchased land; as established Catholic landowners, they successfully fought a legal battle that established their right to stay.

By the 1830s, the relentless western flow of settlers had reached Lake Michigan. With the completion of the Erie Canal in 1825 and the Welland Canal in 1829, Niagara Falls was finally bypassed, opening the Great Lakes area to easy water access. Early roads, following ancient Indian trails, were built in the Lake Michigan area in the 1820s and 1830s. By the 1840s, rail transportation systems reached the lake.

Lake Michigan was fast becoming a true ethnic and cultural "melting pot," as a flood of European immigrants began to arrive in the late 1840s. They came with dreams of land, of opportunity, and of relief from economic depression, famine, and religious persecution. With them they brought their skills in fishing, farming, and lumbering; when necessary, they adapted and learned new skills required by a new land.

From northern Europe they came to the Door Peninsula: Norwegians, Danes, and Icelanders to Washington Island; Swedes to Sister Bay; Norwegian Moravians to Ephraim; Belgians to Brussels, Namur, and Dyckesville. Perhaps they were attracted by a climate similar to that of northern Europe, which allowed them to use familiar grains and agricultural methods. Perhaps the cliffs, North Woods, and open water reminded them of home.

To the mouth of the Black River (later renamed Macatawa River) came Dutch immigrants—dissenters from the established Dutch church who, like the earlier Pilgrims, were seeking freedom from religious persecution. In 1847 they founded Holland, Michigan. Accustomed to working in a wetland environment, the

The "long ship" Paterson *plies the waters of the Manitou Passage.*

hardworking Dutch became successful farmers in the wetland-rich west Michigan area. According to historian Milo Quaife, "Holland has become the foremost center of Dutch cultural influence in America." Today the annual Tulip Festival celebrates Dutch customs and dress through a variety of celebrations.

And so Lake Michigan lured immigrants from all over Europe: Germany, the British Isles, Scandinavia, and southern and eastern European countries. American-born settlers came too, including those of African and Spanish descent. The lake provided a wide variety of potential jobs in shipping, fishing, farming, and logging, and in laboring in iron mines, quarries, and growing industries. New towns were springing up all around the lakeshore. Rapidly growing Chicago was becoming a vital hub in the nation's transportation systems.

To build these new towns and cities required lumber, and the supply of timber, especially white pine, seemed endless in the surrounding forests. The need for lumber created a lumbering boom that in turn brought new workers to the area: lumberjacks, camp workers, sawmill operators, and crews of great

lumber-carrying schooners. Lake Michigan and its many tributary rivers aided in the harvest of its surrounding timber, floating logs downstream to sawmills and transporting lumber from sawmills to Chicago. This booming city became the nation's largest lumber market, the center of the lumber delivery system.

Lumbering reigned around Lake Michigan from the 1850s to the early 1900s. Local legends still spin colorful tales of sawdust towns, lumber camps, and the hardy lumberjacks themselves. But it was strenuous and hazardous work — from felling the giant trees and hauling them to the river, to maneuvering the mass of pitching and rolling logs downriver. Billions of board-feet of lumber reached lakeside mills in these river-borne log drives. In the 1870s, railroads were increasingly used to transport logs from forest to mill, and allowed the lumberjacks to reach deeper into the forests from the rivers and streams.

By 1900, most of Lake Michigan's pine was gone. Just as it had been impossible to comprehend the finiteness of the supply of beaver pelts in the vast forests, so an end to the forest itself had been inconceivable. Lumber barons were proud of the scope of their achieve-

Lake Michigan has long fulfilled a number of human needs, including recreation.

ment. Well over 70 billion boardfeet of lumber was harvested from Lake Michigan's watersheds. They did not realize the environmental price that was paid. Left behind were vast tracts of land laid waste, barren but for stumps and slash. Wildlife habitats were devastated, in forests, streams, rivers, and Lake Michigan.

But the most dramatic and immediate consequences were the frequent forest fires of 1870 to 1920. Most infamous is the Great Chicago Fire of October 8, 1871, which started in the O'Leary barn. Fueled by strong winds, the blaze ravaged three and one half square miles of the city. Panic ensued. People leapt from burning buildings; the streets and bridges were overwhelmed by panic-stricken residents fleeing the rushing flames. Many sought refuge in the shallow waters of Lake Michigan. Estimates list 300 lives lost, 17,000 buildings destroyed, and one-third of Chicago's 300,000 people left homeless. In retrospect, Chicago had been especially vulnerable to fire. Most of the homes and businesses were wooden, built from Michi-

gan and Wisconsin lumber. Even the pine sidewalks were combustible. And so in the Chicago fire, nature ironically took back what had been wrested from her.

But the Chicago fire is only a small part of a much greater story. That same night, a series of devastating fires nearly encircled Lake Michigan. The area had been ripe for disaster. Lumbering had left piles of dry slash littering the forest floor. The fastest way to clear land for farming was by the torch, which left isolated fires burning throughout the region. Add to these the campfires left smoldering by logging camps and railroad construction camps, and a long, severe drought in the fall of 1871.

The powerful southwest winds of October 8 and 9 whipped isolated fires into a spectacular conflagration that raged across the land. This blaze fed on itself, as rising and swirling currents of air within the flames created a fire tornado that bore down upon the little town of Peshtigo, Wisconsin. Over eight hundred people died as Peshtigo was totally destroyed in less than an hour. The Peshtigo River afforded safe haven to many of those who managed to survive the holocaust. They lived to tell tales of horror — of the deafening crashing and booming that announced the onslaught of the fire storm, of trees exploding in flames, of family and friends instantly cremated before their eyes.

Devastating as the Peshtigo Fire was, there was still more. The fire raged on towards Menominee, while across Green Bay the Door Peninsula was also ablaze. On Lake Michigan's western shores that night, more than 1,100 lives were lost, and over a million acres of land left in ashes. At the same time, flames swept across the Stonington Peninsula, the Garden Peninsula, along Little and Big Bays De Noc. And Lake Michigan's east coast was afire for hundreds of miles. Holland and Manistee were consumed, while firefighters in South Haven and Muskegon just managed to fend off total destruction. The conflagration spread across Michigan's lower peninsula all the way to Lake Huron's shores. At least 2 ½ million acres of Michigan timberland burned that night. Wildlife suffered death and destruction of their habitats — including fish, as lakes and streams were overheated, and poisoned by toxic run-off from the widespread ashes.

A century later, the healing of our remaining forestland is well under way. Through reforestation efforts in the 1930s, along with nature's own revitalization processes, our state and national forests are again alive with life. But only in a few places can we see the rare giant, ancient survivors of the logging boom: virgin hardwoods at Warren Woods, Michigan; five-hundred-year-old virgin white cedars in South Manitou Island's Valley of the Giants; virgin white pines at Michigan's Interlochen State Park and Hartwick Pines State Park.

Another Lake Michigan resource eagerly sought by its new inhabitants was its fish. Tales of Indians and early settlers described waters teeming with whitefish, lake trout, herring, and sturgeon. With the influx of settlers into the region, a market for commercial fishing grew. In 1875, Lake Michigan fishermen harvested nearly 12 million pounds of fish. Five years later, that number had nearly doubled. But, as with beaver pelts and timber, this resource proved it was not infinite; and so the commercial fishing industry suffered a host of ills brought on by human overuse of Lake Michigan's fish and their watery environment.

At the same time that Lake Michigan's fish and timber resources were proving so valuable to the growth of America's heartland, the lake was instrumental in the boom of industrial growth that transformed the nation into a world-class industrial power. Surrounded by all the natural resources necessary for steel production, the Great Lakes provided the vital water transportation to bring these components together. From Lake Michigan's shores came limestone; from south and east of the lake came coal; just north of Lake Michigan lay vast ranges of iron ore, reaching across Michigan's western Upper Peninsula into northern Wisconsin and Minnesota. Steel plants sprang up at the south end of Lake Michigan, growing and sprawling until they became one of the largest concentrations of heavy industry in the world.

Iron ore has been shipped over Lake Michigan since 1865, reaching the lakeshore by rail from the Marquette, Menominee, and Gogebic ranges. To cut transportation costs, ore was converted to pig iron in charcoal-fired blast furnaces at many Lake Michigan locations: Green Bay, Menominee, Escanaba, Fayette, Manistique, St. Ignace, Leland, Frankfort, and Grand Haven. At Fayette, the Jackson Iron Company established a company town that prospered from 1867 until the 1880s, when hardwoods to fuel the furnaces became scarce. After smelting nearly 230,000 tons of pig iron, the Fayette furnaces closed at the end of 1890. Today this "ghost town" is being restored as the focus of Michigan's Fayette State Park.

Fleets of ore-carrying ships were built; by 1900, ore freighters were as long as 435 feet and carried more than 6,000 tons. In the 20th century, these "long ships" have evolved into 1,000-foot-long self-unloading supercarriers. Today these huge ships still ply the waters of Lake Michigan — quite a contrast to the birchbark supercarriers of only a few centuries ago.

And what of the Native Americans who inhabited the land for thousands of years? Despite overwhelming adversity, they have endured, with a remarkable will to survive. Indian communities and reservations remain around Lake Michigan and her sister Great Lakes. Many traditions and beliefs of their ancient culture have also endured. Finally, we are just beginning to view their ancient understandings of living in harmony with the natural world, not in the usual romantic and trivializing sense, but as timeless realities with enduring significance in modern contexts.

Humans arrived at the shores of ancestral Lake Michigan soon after her postglacial birth, and our histories have unfolded simultaneously, intricately intertwined. People have witnessed the lake's life evolving — her many moods, her spirit. Over the ages, her waters have nurtured us, buoyed our vessels, and shared her resources with us — guiding our own development. As we face the future together, Lake Michigan and her human inhabitants remain interdependent and connected, together a part of an ever-evolving creation.

MARITIME TALES

I have seen the storms of the Channel, those of the Ocean, the squalls off the banks of New-foundland, those on the coasts of America, and the hurricanes of the Gulf of Mexico. No where have I witnessed the fury of the elements comparable to that found on this fresh water sea.
— Francis Count de Castelnau, 1842

French naturalist Count de Castelnau, "assailed by a frightful storm" in the Manitou Passage, survived to testify to the awesome power Lake Michigan can wield. Experienced Great Lakes sailors know the ominous potential of this wild lake — equal to, and sometimes greater than, that of saltwater oceans. The term "lake" belies the true nature of this inland freshwater sea.

Lake Michigan has its own rich maritime heritage, replete with tales of tragic shipwrecks in howling gales, of ships that sailed away without a trace, of sunken wrecks laden with treasure, of fire and collisions. For 9,000 years, these waters have been a highway for human travel and adventure, from prehistoric Indian canoes to modern supercarriers.

Shipping traffic reached its peak in the 19th century. The rudimentary roads of the day could not compete with the ease and accessibility of water travel. And so Lake Michigan provided the main highway system — but one without signs, traffic lights, established routes, or well-defined "rules of the road." Vessels crisscrossed the lake, often at high speed and occasionally without running lights. Tragedy was inevitable, especially when storms or fog were added to the equation.

Under the auspices of the U.S. Lighthouse Service, navigational aids were constructed along Lake Michigan's shorelines. Lighthouse beacons warned of obstacles to shipping (shoals, reefs, islands) and guided the way in fair and foul weather. The U.S. Lifesaving Service established lifesaving stations that dotted the coastline. Their crews manned lookout towers, patrolled the beaches in fog and darkness, and lighted signal flares to warn ships straying too near shore. When shipwrecks occurred, surfmen jeopardized their lives to bring in survivors — using beach apparatus that often had to be hauled miles to the site, or venturing out onto stormy seas in open surfboats.

Modern navigational technology has improved safety on the seas, but even today's lake freighters are not immune to the fury of the lake's wind and waves. Such was the case of the 640-foot-long limestone carrier *Carl D. Bradley.* At one time the longest vessel on the Great Lakes, her hull of riveted steel plates had been considered "unsinkable, the safest vessel afloat on the inland seas." On November 18, 1958, west of the Beaver Island group, a fierce gale whipped up twenty-foot waves intermittently cresting to thirty feet. With a sudden ominous thud, the ship's long deck humped and sagged. Crewmen were thrown overboard as the ship rolled and heaved. The *Bradley*'s stern rose high above them, then plunged straight down with a tremendous explosion as the ship's boilers went under. The ensuing long perilous night of search and rescue efforts was nearly futile; only two crewmen survived, enduring the freezing night on a small life raft.

Storms are not the only danger to Lake Michigan mariners. Many a ship has been destroyed by fire —

The skeletal remains of the J. Hazard Hartzell *appear and disappear, according to the shifting sands and water levels of Lake Michigan. The schooner ran aground in a sudden storm in October 1880, near Elberta.*

started by human carelessness, faulty machinery, lightning, and even airborne cinders from forest fires. For two decades, smoke from frequent forest fires created a choking fog in which ships collided with the shore, shoals, and each other. In the Straits of Mackinac on the night of the Chicago and Peshtigo fires of 1871, thick smoke eliminated visibility. James Davenport kept a solitary vigil at Waugoshance Lighthouse; for three days, he continuously rang his fog bell, holding pans in one hand to awaken him when he drifted to sleep and dropped them.

Low visibility is more commonly caused by fog, hazardous even in the age of modern navigational technology. On foggy May 6, 1965, the 504-foot *Upson* blindly rammed the lighthouse station at Gray's Reef; both ship and lighthouse escaped severe damage. The next morning, the blanket of fog over the Straits continued its havoc with shipping, as the *Cedarville* and

Topdalsfjord collided. Ten crewmen perished when the *Cedarville* sank two miles from shore.

Ironically, what has been described as the "greatest of all disasters in the history of the Great Lakes" was caused by human error, and happened only a few feet from shore. On July 24, 1915, the excursion liner *Eastland* capsized in the Chicago River as she pulled away from the dock, drowning 835 passengers. The catastrophe has been attributed to overcrowding passengers beyond capacity, and to instability due to improper filling of water-ballast tanks.

Certainly human error has played a role in many maritime tragedies. But when fogbanks cause lake freighters to collide, when the pounding of wind and wave dashes foundering ships onto unseen reefs, or when towering waves break the back of a giant such as the *Bradley,* we are reminded of Lake Michigan's wild and unpredictable nature.

Freshwater waves are different than saltwater waves. Less dense, they are sharper and strike faster, leaving little time for a ship to recover from one blow to the next. On the Great Lakes, there is little "sea room" in which to ride out a long storm, with numerous obstacles—islands, shoals, mainland shores, and other vessels in busy shipping lanes. When winds sweep the length of Lake Michigan, mountainous waves can build, powerful enough to break up a great ore freighter.

   The North Pier Lights at St. Joseph, Michigan guide boaters into the St. Joseph River. The first two lights on Lake Michigan were built in 1832 at Chicago and St. Joseph. The mouth of the St. Joseph River was also the site of the earliest recorded navigational aid on Lake Michigan. Here in 1679, La Salle's men waited in vain for the Griffon, *and Father Louis Hennepin wrote: "We sounded the mouth of the river and discovered a sand bar there. To aid the entrance of our ship, in case it arrived, we marked the channel by two tall poles with bear skin pendants." But the* Griffon *had already sailed into oblivion, to become the first of Lake Michigan's "Flying Dutchmen."*

Cana Island Lighthouse is one of more than seventy–five lighthouse towers still remaining on Lake Michigan, standing as monuments to the lives and dramas that unfolded about them.

Porte des Morts ("Death's Door"), the passage through a group of rocky islands into Green Bay, received its name from early French explorers and fur traders. Legends tell of more than one hundred Indians in canoes caught in a sudden squall and dashed against the rocks of Porte des Morts. At the entrance to Porte des Morts, Pilot Island Lighthouse is said to have witnessed more shipwrecks than any other lighthouse on the Great Lakes. The diary of keeper Martin Knudsen in the late 1800s indicated shipwrecks at least twice a week. In one week of 1872, nearly one hundred vessels were damaged or destroyed while passing through Death's Door.

Under the waters of Lake Michigan lie the bones of countless ships overwhelmed by confusing currents, heavy winds, high seas, or blinding fog. Some of these hidden wrecks are said to be laden with riches, including a fortune of $5 million supposedly lying on the bottom near Poverty Island. Tales of such sunken treasures have lured many a scuba diver on unsuccessful searches. In the mid–1800s, a project was seriously considered that would dam up the Straits and drain the lake, all to facilitate retrieval of legendary treasures. Fortunately the idea, which totally underestimated the magnitude of this inland sea, never caught on. And the lake continues to conceal her mysteries of the deep.

On November 29, 1960, the Liberian steamer Francisco Morazon *was stranded off South Manitou Island in a heavy gale; all the crew were rescued by a Coast Guard helicopter. The ship's broken form still lies offshore. The Morazon's size makes it appear deceivingly close, but the swim from shore dispels this deception. Bobbing in the gentle lake swells, we swam alongside the partially sunken wreck, its immense hulk looming above us. Peering into the depths below, and exploring further by snorkeling, we gazed on submerged pieces of the ship's bow, broken and twisted. Above us, the ship's present crew of nesting gulls and cormorants watched us curiously, their cries filling the air. The cormorants' vulturelike forms added to the foreboding eeriness of the scene. Dwarfed by the massive ruins all about us, we could only begin to imagine the awesome scenes witnessed by survivors of even more disastrous shipwrecks than this one — mountainous waves that twist, fracture, and swallow leviathans much larger than the* Francisco Morazon.

 While the lake boasts a long and rich maritime history, many smaller, historically insignificant dramas unfold daily. Our first trip to North Manitou Island brought such an unexpected drama. We had hitched a ride to the island in a friend's powerboat, cruised along the shore, and hiked inland to camp overnight. The next afternoon, severe storm warnings on the radio prompted a quick departure. Before we were halfway to Frankfort on the mainland, streaks of lightning appeared on the western horizon. Darkness arrived early that night, carried by the approaching storm. The bolts grew brighter and larger; thunder rumbled about us. Suddenly the radio warned: "All boats get off the lake! Now!" Good advice, but not always possible. We were an hour from any harbor of refuge, and our only option was to keep going.

 The light had gone out in the boat's compass, so we aimed for Point Betsie Light. In the darkness we sped toward that beacon, depending totally on its guidance, as sailors had for over a century. It was a wildly beautiful scene—the lighthouse beam cut steadfastly through the darkness, while jagged lightning bolts streaked above the tower. We reached Frankfort safely, entering the breakwaters just as the squall line brought powerful gusts of wind and a torrential downpour.

 Lake Michigan's long history of maritime tragedies, lighthouses, and lifesaving stations was certainly on our minds that evening. In spite of modern technology, Lake Michigan still imparts her surprises, and there are still people tossed about in small boats on stormy seas—thankful to follow the path of a lighthouse's beacon to safe haven.

REDISCOVERING
THE WILD

WILDERNESS REMNANTS

Let us probe the silent places, let us seek what luck betide us;
Let us journey to a lonely land I know.
There's a whisper on the night-wind, there's a star agleam to guide us,
And the Wild is calling, calling . . . let us go.

— Robert Service

Only three centuries ago, the entire North American continent was an uncharted wilderness; humans lived within its realm, but left little impact. To these Native Americans, the natural world was not wild—it was home. Today, human endeavors dominate the majority of our landscapes; pristine wilderness has become a rare and fleeting thing—so rare that modern people find themselves embroiled in debates about the intrinsic value of wilderness, and even how it should be recognized and defined. While dictionaries still list one definition of wilderness as "barren wasteland," our society is beginning to recognize the inherent, priceless value of wilderness. The Wilderness Act of 1964 recognized wilderness as "an area where the earth and its community of life are untrammeled by man, where man himself is a visitor who does not remain."

Lake Michigan, with the largest human population of all the Great Lakes, has but a handful of areas that have received official federal wilderness designation and its accompanying protection under this milestone law. For the most part, Lake Michigan's wild areas are isolated vestiges of an ancient unbroken wilderness. This patchwork of wilderness remnants varies greatly—from nearly untouched remote areas to smaller tracts that, while exhibiting the scars of human impact, still offer an important touch of the wild. And the lake itself, though not untouched by people, remains wild and untamed. To an extent, this inland sea is the quintessential wilderness, for our passing leaves no footprints.

Our search for the wild areas of Lake Michigan has been a joyful family adventure, one we highly recommend. Clearly the best way to fully appreciate the magnitude and beauty of this inland sea is to experience it firsthand. The following discussion of Lake Michigan's wilderness remnants is by no means complete; rather, it is intended to give readers a starting point for their own Lake Michigan explorations.

Several types of natural areas are available for public enjoyment. Under the auspices of the National Park Service, two national lakeshores—Indiana Dunes and Sleeping Bear Dunes—preserve magnificent natural areas, and offer a wide range of recreational and learning opportunities. Each state bordering Lake Michigan features the lakeshore in one or more state parks. Recreational activities are also available in the state and national forests bordering the lake—often with less crowded, and more scenic, campgrounds, and a better chance to find solitude.

Besides federal and state land, certain private preserves are open to the public. The Nature Conservancy has been a leader in rescuing unique land from development. Its solution is a simple one: Buy it. With funds from supporters around the world, this group is "dedicated to preserving natural areas that represent a

Grand Mere State Park.

true diversity in plant and animal life" by identifying endangered ecosystems, protecting them (often by purchase), and arranging for their future preservation. Many significant preserves on Lake Michigan exist today because of the efforts of the Nature Conservancy, especially the Wisconsin and Michigan chapters. Many of these ecosystems are fragile and cannot tolerate crowds of visitors, however well-meaning. Thus, instead of listing specific preserves here, we encourage interested readers to contact the chapters for more information.

The Nature Conservancy is not alone in its conservation efforts. Many other nature preserves around Lake Michigan have been established through the dedicated efforts of other conservation groups, as well as nature associations, centers, and clubs. No matter how small or large the package, remnants of the wild protected by these groups contribute to the important remaining patchwork.

INDIANA DUNES NATIONAL LAKESHORE

Compared with the less settled northern regions, Lake Michigan's South Basin has more sparsely distributed wilderness remnants, making them all the more precious. Along the coasts of Indiana, Illinois, and southern Wisconsin lies a spreading, sprawling metropolitan area; this urban network incorporating cities, suburbs, and industries from Gary to Milwaukee has been described as a "single, giant megalopolis." Sprinkled throughout these municipalities are little islands of nature refuges, where city dwellers can find renewal in these microcosms of water and wind, forest and shore.

The largest of these "islands" in the midst of civilization is Indiana Dunes National Lakeshore, the lonely surviving fragments of great dunes that once rimmed Lake Michigan's southern shore. Over the ages, these ever-shifting dunes were witness to a stream of activity. Indians passed silently on foot along major trails. Stagecoaches rolled along the lakeshore — winding around the hills of sand, along the packed wet beach, and even out into the water, following a curving sandbar to cross the mouth of the Calumet River. Early experiments in flight were launched from these dunes; in hundreds of flights, Octave Chanute developed a biplane glider that was modified and motorized by the Wright Brothers a few years later. And then the overwhelming onrush of industrialization arrived. Dunes were leveled, wetlands filled, harbors dredged, and the Calumet River relocated. The vast, sandy wilderness became a crowded expanse of cement and smokestacks, factories and homes, oil refineries and steel plants — according to environmental writer William Ashworth, "probably the world's largest single concentration of heavy industry."

The Indiana Dunes were rescued from this relentless press of development largely through a campaign started in the early 1900s by the Prairie Club of Chicago (with such notable members as Carl Sandburg and Jane Addams). The creation of Indiana Dunes State Park in 1923 saved 2,200 acres; in 1966, Indiana Dunes National Lakeshore was created, our country's first urban national park. Today the park encompasses more than 13,000 acres, including fourteen miles of beach between Michigan City and Gary.

Indiana Dunes National Lakeshore is actually a patchwork of several separate parcels, or units. The state park, though included within the national lakeshore boundaries, is still managed by the Indiana state park system. Confusing? This can all be sorted out by stopping first at the park headquarters. Which park? Take your pick — headquarters for both the state park and national lakeshore are located in Chesterton, Indiana.

Though only a fragment of the original expanse of dunes, both parks offer a wide variety of excellent dune habitat to explore: beaches, bare foredunes, interdunal wetlands, and hardwood dunes. A network of interconnecting trails winds through the state park, covering sixteen and a half miles; and there are campgrounds, picnic areas, and a swimming beach. The national lakeshore offers four swimming beaches, a visitor center, and twenty-seven miles of trails (twelve separate hiking trails and one bicycle trail).

The Indiana Dunes have attracted millions of visitors, which says a lot for the need this work of nature must be meeting; but at the same time, this popularity decreases the chance of finding solitude and quiet. However, most of the crowds throng to the beaches. Hiking the longer trails, you escape the boom boxes. The farther you go, and the deeper the sand, the better the solitude. The dunes' close proximity to heavy industry makes a striking contrast; it also reduces the wildness of the experience, as the hum of industrial machinery and the sulfur smell from smokestacks are rarely absent. Visually, however, the wonderful array of dune and wetland communities provides a window into the area's wild past.

ILLINOIS BEACH STATE PARK

The only dunes in Illinois are featured in Illinois Beach State Park, tucked in between Waukegan and Zion. Stretching a total of six miles along the lakeshore, the two park units make up the only Illinois state park on Lake Michigan. While the beach and modest dunes are the dominating features, nature trails lead hikers through prairie, marshland, forest, and of course, sand dunes.

Indiana Dunes National Lakeshore.

Illinois Beach State Park.

Chiwaukee Prairie.

CHIWAUKEE PRAIRIE

Just north of the Illinois-Wisconsin border (between Chicago and Milwaukee — hence its name) lies a rare remnant of the vast prairies that once carpeted the area. This "primeval sanctuary" has been described by the Wisconsin Nature Conservancy, instrumental in its preservation, as "the last unbroken stretch of prairie of its kind in the state, home to more than 400 native plant species." The rich diversity of plants thriving among the swaying prairie grasses is remarkable, and includes many rare species. Part of this diversity is supported by alternating low ridges and swales of the beach ridge complex, which create a variety of habitats: dry sandy prairie, wet prairie, marshland, fens, and open-grown oaks.

Looking toward Lake Michigan, the view is interrupted by power lines and homes dotted along the shore, reminders of how near civilization lies. In spite of this visual intrusion, the sweeping open spaces, expanses of color, and subtle scents of the prairie are refreshing and inspiring. Chiwaukee Prairie's 226 acres have received protection through designation as a national natural landmark and a state natural area.

SOUTHERN MICHIGAN STATE PARKS

Along Lake Michigan's southeastern coast are a series of Michigan state parks that share many similarities, including vistas of towering dunes and white expanses of first-rate swimming beaches. Beginning only ten miles north of the Indiana border, this broken chain of state parks stretches along the coast: Warren Dunes, Grand Mere, Van Buren, Saugatuck Dunes, Holland, Grand Haven, P.J. Hoffmaster, and Muskegon. These are popular summer attractions, and solitude is best found by hiking the longest trails.

The magnificent dunes gracing these coastal parks are featured especially well at P.J. Hoffmaster State Park, just south of Muskegon. At the Gillette Nature Center are excellent opportunities for learning about dune ecology through dramatic slide presentations, dioramas, interpretive exhibits, and a hands-on area for children (and others young at heart). The center is the base for many nature-oriented activities throughout the seasons, including the Trillium Festival in May.

The newest of the southern Michigan state parks is Grand Mere, set aside from development through long efforts of the Grand Mere Association and the

P.J. Hoffmaster State Park.

Nature Conservancy. Grand Mere, designated a national natural landmark area, features a unique combination of Lake Michigan shore, bare and wooded dunes, three interdunal lakes, and a swamp. This diverse environment is home to many waterfowl, a profusion of wildflowers, and rare and endangered plant species.

Grand Mere is a day-use park, with no camping and few other facilities, but this lack of development helps preserve the park's character. We have been fortunate to live near Grand Mere, with its renewing spirit accessible by a quick drive or bicycle ride. There we can escape the busy sounds of U.S. Interstate Highway 94 traffic on the far side of a mountain of sand, where auditory intrusions are overwhelmed by the relentless surf. After a January morning hike at Grand Mere, John wrote in his diary:

Standing in leaves, I heard the rapid sound of many small footsteps coming over the hardwood dune. Two red foxes, one chasing the other, bounded over the hill approximately thirty feet away; they continued over the next dune, the sound of their footfalls in the leaves trailing after them. They paid no atten-

tion to me, but they were the event of my day.

TENSION ZONE (WISCONSIN)

Several Wisconsin state parks lie in the vicinity of the Tension Zone, where two environmentally contrasting regions interface. On the northern edge of this transitional zone, Harrington Beach State Park, a day-use park at the site of an old limestone quarry, features an inland quarry lake, nature trails, and Lake Michigan beach. Kohler-Andrae State Park, just south of Sheboygan, offers sand dunes, hiking trails (including a protective cordwalk over fragile dunes), nearly two miles of beach, the Sanderling Nature Center, and family camping.

Native Americans inhabited this area from early prehistoric times. Evidences of the region's rich ancient history can still be seen nearby. The works of Effigy Mound builders are preserved at Sheboygan Indian Mound Park just to the north, and Lizard Mound Park at West Bend. To the west, the works of glaciers can be seen at Kettle Moraine State Forest, Northern Unit.

Over 15,000 years ago, a thick ice mass covered the Lake Michigan area, including three-fourths of Wisconsin. Despite their slow movement, the massive glaciers wielded a relentless power in remolding the landscape. The Green Bay Lobe and Lake Michigan Lobe of the Wisconsinan Glacier reached southward and gradually expanded; when they met, these two giant fingers of ice ground against each other, then merged. The eventual retreat of the ice wall from this glacial skirmish zone left a concentrated region of Ice Age landforms: moraines, kames, drumlins, eskers, kettles, outwash plains.

These glacial handiworks can be found throughout the Lake Michigan region, but the Kettle Moraine area contains an outstanding assemblage. To protect these unique features and preserve this natural heritage, the Ice Age National Scientific Reserve was created. Several different Ice Age units lie along the terminal moraine of the Wisconsinan Glacier. The partially completed Ice Age Trail will eventually link these units and lead hikers across Wisconsin along nearly 1,000 miles of the winding moraine.

The Northern Unit of Kettle Moraine State Forest encompasses over 20,000 acres north of Milwaukee and west of Sheboygan and Port Washington. A guidebook available at the Ice Age Visitor Center takes visitors on an enlightening self-guided auto tour through forty miles of scenic forest roads, explaining geologic features along the way. Camping is available at family campgrounds on Long Lake and Mauthe Lake, and in backpacking shelters scattered along the Ice Age Trail. You experience the glacial features most intimately by hiking this trail—following the ups and downs of the rolling terrain, surmounting high ridgetops, and curving along serpentine eskers.

TENSION ZONE (MICHIGAN)

Michigan's P.J. Hoffmaster State Park lies in the Tension Zone; because of this unique position, plant and animal species of both northern and southern ecological zones may be seen there. For example, this area is the southernmost nesting location for the northern goshawk, and the northernmost area where black rat snakes are found. In dune areas to the south of the park, oaks are dominant, while at Hoffmaster white cedars begin asserting themselves in a mixed beech-maple-hemlock forest.

To the north, at Silver State Park, towering white sand dunes bordering Silver Lake give striking contrast to the blue of water and sky. On the Lake Michigan beach, the tall red brick tower of Little Point Sable Lighthouse rises picturesquely from the dunes. People seem especially drawn to this scenic spot. One evening near sunset we watched as visitors arrived at the lighthouse—wandering barefoot along the shore, or hiking from the nearby parking area over the dunes. They spoke quietly in small groups, flew kites, and played. But as the sun neared the horizon and the sky glowed its deep crimson hues, all sat and watched in silence. The sunball seemed to grow in size, with fluid margins, then flattened as it sank and disappeared. Once the sun extinguished itself, the onlookers turned almost as a group towards the lighthouse, as if waiting for something. Minutes later, the bright rays of the beacon beamed across the darkening water. Spontaneously, many applauded, before quietly departing.

LUDINGTON STATE PARK

Nestled between Hamlin Lake and Lake Michigan is Ludington State Park, just north of the town of Ludington. Although one of Michigan's most popular state parks, this wilderness remnant has enough space (4,514 acres) for people to find solitude and unspoiled vistas. Miles of magnificent Lake Michigan beach stretch north to Big Sable Point, guarded by the tall, black-and-white tower of Big Point Sable Lighthouse. In a hike along the shore to the lighthouse, the bleached bones of an old wooden sailing ship at the water's edge may or may not reveal themselves, depending on the waves and water level. The hide-and-seek game of this old shipwreck mirrors the lake's capricious nature.

Exploring the dunes that line the shore and spread inland may reveal other wild wonders. Deer often fleetingly appear and disappear, moving silently between dunes and through the forest. Evidence of the North Woods' increasing hold on the land manifests itself in the greater mix of conifers on wooded dunes. Interspersed throughout the sandy landscape are isolated little wetlands. The winding Big Sable River often fills with Canada geese, a variety of ducks, and their raucous, welcome music.

The view from Big Sable Point is sweeping. To the west, an inland sea stretches to the horizon. To both the south and north reach seemingly endless spans of beach and dunes. The northward view is especially rare—an uninterrupted procession of wild, shifting sand dunes. These are the Nordhouse Dunes. Together the shores of Ludington State Park and Nordhouse Dunes Wilderness Area encompass twelve miles of undeveloped Lake Michigan duneland.

NORDHOUSE DUNES WILDERNESS AREA

With the Michigan Wilderness Act of 1987, Nordhouse Dunes joined a few Michigan and Wisconsin wildlife refuge islands as the only federally designated wilderness areas on Lake Michigan. This 3,450-acre parcel of undeveloped dunes in the Manistee National Forest gained its wilderness status through long efforts of a number of individuals and groups, including the Sierra Club and Nature Conservancy. Accord-

Dundee Mountain is a prominent glacial feature at Kettle Moraine State Forest, Northern Unit. The hill was formed by accumulated debris from a stream of meltwater flowing through a hole in the massive sheet of ice.

Little Point Sable Lighthouse, Silver Lake State Park.

ing to the Nature Conservancy, the Nordhouse Dunes area "contains the most extensive interdunal wetlands on the Great Lakes and is one of the highest quality examples of a sand dune ecosystem. The open dunes are probably the most extensive windblown dunes on a freshwater lake in the world." A publication of Michigan's Sierra Club reported that "the Nordhouse Dunes/Ludington State Park area is the largest tract of publicly owned, relatively undisturbed dune associated land in the United States, and possibly in the world."

At the north edge of the Wilderness Area is Lake Michigan Recreation Area, which contains facilities for camping, picnicking, and swimming. The four campground loops (aptly named Violet, Oak, Orchid, and Hemlock) are less congested and less trampled than most state park campgrounds. In springtime, we found wild orchids growing within a few feet of the parking space at our campsite; the soft calls of whippoorwills lulled us to sleep that night. And on a cold, crisp autumn night, we were serenaded in our tent by the high, wavering songs of nearby coyotes.

To experience the wilderness qualities of Nordhouse Dunes requires some effort. A network of sandy trails enters the Wilderness Area from both its north and south edges; the initial portions of these trails are

more heavily used. Hiking in the yielding sand can be exhausting, especially with a loaded backpack. As one hiker described it: "You take two steps forward and sink one step backward." On the open dunes, the sun's heat is intensified by reflection off the sand. Add sand accumulating in hiking boots, and it is clear why the crowds disappear the farther down the trail you go. It is possible to find rare solitude and quiet among these dunes and shores.

Backpackers have both the freedom to choose their own campsites (except in open dunes or near trails), and the responsibility to use low-impact techniques in the fragile environment. Trails lead through forested dunes, past wetlands, and into the expanse of open dunes. One trail parallels the lakeshore, following ridgetops of high wooded dunes.

The visual beauty of Nordhouse Dunes is made complete by its other sensory gifts. The breeze blowing off the lake cools the skin, and splashing in the chilly water is invigorating. The air smells of moist freshness, and of fragrant pines. Wild blueberries and grapes give welcome refreshment to weary hikers. Pines whisper, loons call from out on the lake, and the cadences of the surf murmur or roar. This rare experience of wholeness is unique to such remote wild places.

LAKE MICHIGAN CAR FERRY

Just south of the wilderness of Nordhouse Dunes and Ludington State Park lies the town of Ludington; here a different kind of wilderness journey begins and ends. The lake itself is a watery wilderness, inaccessible without a boat. One way to experience this inland sea firsthand is by crossing it on the Lake Michigan car ferry, between Ludington and Kewaunee. As this book goes to press, tentative plans are underway to move the Wisconsin port from Kewaunee to Manitowoc.

Clearly, a journey on a 406-foot-long ship using modern navigational equipment and safety features is not a conventional wilderness experience. But the sixty-mile crossing of an inland sea is still an adventure, as it has been through history. The Michigan-Wisconsin Ferry Service now operates the last of a fleet of railroad car ferries that once bridged Lake Michigan, transporting large numbers of railroad cars, automobiles, and passengers between eleven different ports in Michigan and Wisconsin.

On a car ferry voyage, the lake may display one or more of her many moods: the bright blues of a sunny day; the free energy of wind and waves; or the feeling of invisibility in a cloud of fog, accompanied by the ship's deep, rumbling fog horn. Whatever the weather, the journey's high point comes when the land disappears from sight. The scene of endless water in all directions is one to contemplate. This is the same view experienced over the ages by prehistoric Indians, early explorers, fur traders, settlers, sailors on lumber schooners, passengers on excursion steamers, and crews of today's "long ships."

POINT BEACH STATE FOREST

Between Kewaunee and Manitowoc, at the Wisconsin end of the car ferry line, lies Point Beach State Forest, with some 2,800 acres of North Woods and sand-ridged beaches. More than six miles of Lake Michigan shore feature some of the finest beaches found anywhere. (In fact, Wisconsin's entire Lake Michigan shoreline is dotted with wonderful sand beaches in township, city, and state parks.)

Under the waters off Rawley Point lies a graveyard of ships, some thirty vessels wrecked on the treacherous shoals. On shore, Rawley Point Lighthouse continues its lonely vigil, still sending a warning beacon to sailors. Nestled in the forest north of the lighthouse is a peaceful campground, with nicely spaced campsites. As usual, you find the best solitude on the hiking trails, winding along forested ridges, past narrow strips of wetlands, and beside Molash Creek on its way to Lake Michigan.

The drive into Point Beach State Forest from Two Rivers is especially scenic and is designated a Wisconsin rustic road. Driving north along this road one au-

tumn night, we were guided by dancing, pulsating northern lights. Reaching our campsite, we hurried to the beach. There the water reflected the hues of the auroral curtain—hues so strong that they refused to yield even to the bright glow of a full moon.

DOOR PENINSULA

The Door Peninsula is full of variety and contrast. Although its name reflects a history of tragedy in the Porte des Morts Strait ("Death's Door") off its tip, the Door Peninsula today is popular with sailors seeking the beauty and tranquillity of its scenic islands, bays, and harbors. The high precipitous cliffs and headlands of its west coast contrast sharply with the generally low shorelines of the east coast. In Door County, encompassing most of the Door Peninsula, are quaint touristy spots filled with summertime crowds. The developers have arrived, and each small community is struggling to accommodate progress and still retain its unique cultural identity. And so goats still graze on the roof of Al Johnson's Swedish Restaurant, and residents celebrate their heritage in ethnic festivals. In the midst of this hustle and tussle is some of the wildest and most unique beauty in the upper Midwest.

Door County has more shoreline than any county in the United States—240 miles of islands, fjords, wave-cut limestone cliffs, sea caves, cobblestone beaches, stretches of sand, and even dunes. Scenic drives wind past orchards, forests, wildflowers, and panoramas of island and sea. Interspersed among bustling resort towns are a variety of state and county parks that preserve unique wild areas.

Where Sturgeon Bay meets Green Bay, Potawatomi State Park features rolling terrain, steep slopes, limestone cliffs, and a "seascape vista." On the eastern coast of Door County, Whitefish Dunes State Park was created to preserve some of the highest dunes in Wisconsin, along a gently curving sand beach.

Immediately adjacent to this stretch of beach is Cave Point County Park, where sand ends abruptly and rock takes over. Into the lake jut limestone cliffs and ledges, riddled with sea caves carved by waves breaking on underwater shoals. It is said that tunnels in the limestone may create passages under the Door Peninsula, leading to Green Bay. Cave Point visitors, exploring the rocky clifftops, often are unaware that they are above a sea cave until the hollow booming of waves resounds in the cavern, sending reverberations along the cave roof.

Other county parks feature equally dramatic scenes. Ellison Bluff Park offers a striking vision of the sheer limestone cliff and the lake far below. At Door Bluff Headlands, near the western entrance to Porte des Morts, a brief hike down the steep bluff takes visitors to the base of Door Bluff—where cedars cling to

Ludington State Park.

the limestone cliff wall, and the expanse of Lake Michigan stretches to the horizon. We were surprised to find such rugged beauty and solitude in a small county park.

Door County has more lighthouses than any other county on the Great Lakes. One of the most scenic is Cana Island Lighthouse, located on a nine-acre island just offshore between North Bay and Moonlight Bay. Depending on water levels, Cana Island may or may not actually be an island, and a visit may or may not require wet feet. The lighthouse grounds are open to the public at posted hours (the picturesque tower, still in use, is not open for viewing).

A rare natural area of Door County is the Mink River Estuary, described by the Nature Conservancy as "one of the few high quality estuaries remaining in this country." This wetland ecosystem where waters of river and sea meet and mix supports diverse vegetation, and affords important fish spawning grounds and bird migration sites. The Mink River Estuary, called "the most 'pristine' of its kind," begins at spring-fed headwaters and eventually empties into Rowley's Bay. This Nature Conservancy preserve is open to observation by foot or canoe.

PENINSULA STATE PARK

Peninsula State Park is a Door County gem. Occupying a 3,763-acre peninsula, this is one of Wisconsin's first state parks and still among the most popular; yet 77 percent of the park has been designated "essentially undeveloped natural area," where solitude abounds. Peninsula State Park offers many ways to experience its wide-ranging beauty. For motorists, twenty miles of park roads reveal countless shoreline views, dramatic vistas from high bluffs, and sightings of wildlife including deer, raccoon, and blue heron. The park offers nineteen miles of hiking and cross-country skiing trails. The Sunset Bike Trail winds through wetlands and North Woods, and past scenic overlooks. In one section of this trail, bicyclists glide quietly through a cedar grove to the lakeshore—to the west is the bright, island-studded water, and to the east, the dense, cool cedars.

Four family campgrounds contain nearly five hundred campsites, which are usually filled (reservations are strongly recommended). This may sound crowded, but these campgrounds are arranged with privacy and quiet in mind. We applaud camper rule number three: "Noise from your campsite should never be heard on another campsite." Park personnel enforce their rules, and the results have created peaceful camping experiences that are justifiably popular.

Also within Peninsula State Park is the Eagle Bluff Lighthouse, the home of the Duclon family for forty-three years. This historic lighthouse sitting atop a high bluff is now a museum, with guided tours during summer months.

NEWPORT STATE PARK

If Peninsula State Park is a gem, Newport State Park is a diamond in the rough. Near the northern tip of the Door Peninsula, 2,200 acres of hardwood forests, cedar swamps, meadows, and remnants of boreal forest have been designated as wilderness by the Wisconsin Department of Natural Resources. Nearly eleven miles of Lake Michigan shoreline feature rock ledges, sand beaches, and dunes. The park has had minimal development, providing excellent opportunities for hiking (twenty-eight miles of trails), swimming, backpacking, snowshoeing, cross-country skiing, and backpack camping (in all seasons). No motor vehicles are allowed off the blacktop road, and no snowmobiles are allowed in winter.

Sixteen wilderness campsites requiring hikes of one to three miles offer backpackers secluded havens in an environment of lakeshore and North Woods. During winter, Newport State Park is one of those rare places where campers do not experience the intrusion of snowmobiles near remote campsites. At Newport, packing in by ski or snowshoe is rewarded by priceless wilderness experiences. On a January camping trip, Ann wrote in her diary:

Awakening early, I left behind snoring bundles of sleeping bags in the tent, as I rose to meet the dawn. A diffuse pinkness glowed gently on sky and snow—a foot of new-fallen powder blanketed everything, in a world of softness and silence. At the shoreline beneath puffy lumps of snow lay slumbering rocks. Beyond the ice cover of our small cove stretched the open water; there mergansers cruised and dived, surrounded by wisps of rising steam fog. Only the occasional groans of shifting ice broke the stillness. In the cold and silence, time seemed suspended.

The words of Sigurd Olson came to mind: "I think the loss of quiet in our lives is one of the great tragedies of civilization, and to have known even for a moment the silence of the wilderness is one of our most precious memories."

Eventually, the sun rose and transformed everything into bright hues of white and blue—creating a different kind of beauty. A fishing boat appeared on the horizon; across the bay drifted the sounds of slushy ice moving against the boat's hull, and the faint "chucka-chucka-chucka" of the boat's engine. These distant, gentle sounds were the only sounds of civilization we heard that wintry morning at Newport State Park. But I especially treasure those timeless moments before dawn—a time of silence and pastel softness.

RIDGES SANCTUARY

On the Door Peninsula between Baileys Harbor Bay and Moonlight Bay, the Ridges Sanctuary was

Nordhouse Dunes Wilderness Area.

The showy lady's slipper is the official flower of the orchid-rich Ridges Sanctuary.

created to preserve the rich ecological communities of a series of parallel, alternating sandy ridges and marshy swales. This complex represents a succession of ancient shorelines formed by currents, wind, and changing lake levels. Ridge formation continues today, in sandbars and troughs created as Baileys Harbor Bay slowly fills.

The Ridges Sanctuary harbors twenty-eight species of native orchids and thirteen endangered or threatened plant species. Wetland and bog plants include carnivorous sundews, bladderworts, and pitcher plants. Winds blowing off the lake create a cool, moist environment where remnants of the boreal forest ecosystem thrive: lichens and mosses; conifers such as spruces, tamaracks, and the fragrant balsam fir; and flowers and herbs, including arctic primrose, Labrador tea, twinflower, and many others. Unique to the northern shores of Lake Michigan (and her sister, Lake Huron) is the dwarf lake iris, whose colonies of small blue flowers brighten undisturbed woodland openings in late spring.

Along the ridge crests meander hiking trails that were originally old deer trails. These are narrow foot paths, where wheeled vehicles (including wheelchairs

and baby strollers) are not allowed. Handouts make the rules clear: "The Ridges is a sanctuary where plants and animals come first and people come second. PLEASE STAY ON THE TRAILS." Ridges Sanctuary members patrol the grounds to be of assistance and to enforce their rules. These rules, designed to protect inhabitants from the trampling of thousands of annual visitors, seem strict at first glance. But we soon witnessed the results of a lack of such protection.

Each year in late June, crowds of tourists are drawn by the beauty of Door County's wildflowers—in particular, the Showy Lady's Slipper. This stunning wild orchid freely flaunts its pink and white splendor along county roads, singly and in glorious bunches. We admired and photographed a perfect double-blossom specimen one evening; the next day as we drove by, it was gone. Only a six-inch-wide, three-inch-deep hole remained. Some other admirers had loved it too much. Undoubtedly, it would be taken elsewhere and transplanted into an environment unable to sustain the flower's unique climate and soil requirements (including the necessary soil fungus, *Rhizoctonia*). Someone, in ignorance and greed, had doomed these rare flowers—and deprived everyone

Lake Michigan car ferry.

Rock Island lies off the tip of Washington Island.

Aurora borealis, Point Beach State Forest.

else of their exquisite beauty. (Perhaps, in handling the plant, the thief also discovered it secretes a skin irritant that often causes blistering rashes similar to that of poison ivy!)

Talking with local residents, we learned that such wildflower thievery is apparently common in Door County. But the beauty and character of wild places cannot be uprooted and taken home. And so we are particularly impressed with the careful guardianship of the life within Ridges Sanctuary. The narrow trails stay narrow, and rare wildflowers grow within inches of visitors' passing feet.

ROCK ISLAND STATE PARK

Beyond the northern tip of the Door Peninsula, the infamous Porte des Morts Strait, and tranquil Washington Island lies Rock Island. Although this nine-hundred-acre island is now only seasonally inhabited by state park personnel and campers, it has been a site of human activity over the ages. In a key position along the chain of Niagaran Escarpment islands, Rock Island's sheltered, sandy beach provided a haven for fragile vessels island-hopping across the mouth of Green Bay.

Archaeologists have found evidence of prehistoric occupation as early as 600 B.C. It is believed that, centuries later, Rock Island gave refuge to Hurons, Potawatomis, and other tribes fleeing the wrath of the Iroquois. Accounts from the mid-1600s and early 1700s indicate the presence of a mixed Indian village on an island at the entrance to Green Bay (archaeologic finds indicate this is Rock Island). One described "a small village, composed of people gathered from various nations," which was known for its hospitality and generosity. Most likely, it was in this village that French voyageurs, sent ahead by La Salle to obtain furs from the Native Americans, set up a trading post and awaited the explorer's arrival. After their 1679 rendezvous, their fur-laden cargo ship, the *Griffon,* is believed to have set sail from this point on its final voyage to an unknown fate.

With European settlement, the chain of islands continued to funnel traffic past Rock Island, and it received one of Lake Michigan's earliest lighthouses in 1839. The island was home to Indians, trappers, fishing people, lightkeepers—and eventually an Icelandic-born inventor and electrical equipment manufacturer, Chester H. Thordarson. The island became his private estate, where his philosophy of conservation preserved, undisturbed, all but thirty acres. Stone buildings from the 1920s still stand, reminiscent of Thordarson's Icelandic heritage.

Much like the inland sea encircling it, Rock Island is a place of clear contrasts. It has a significant historical past, yet remains essentially undeveloped. On its north shores rise sheer, unyielding dolomite cliffs; yet the south shore harbors an expanse of soft, yielding sand. Beach views are open, bright, and unobstructed; yet, at the edge of limestone bluffs is the calm and subdued darkness of dense cedar forests. These cedars crowd to the rim, often hanging over the edge and clinging tenaciously to sheer rock faces. Further inland, meadow wildflowers display riots of color, near mature hardwood forests.

Rock Island is only accessible by boat; most visitors arrive via two ferry trips—first from the mainland to Washington Island, then from Washington Island's Jackson Harbor to Rock Island. Camping is primitive, and campers should be prepared to backpack to their sites. No motor vehicles are allowed on the island, according to park literature. (However, the all-terrain vehicle of a ranger making his rounds and an apparently mufflerless park boat were startling auditory intrusions on an otherwise peaceful experience.) The main campground is an easy hike from the ferry dock, and provides scenic and nicely spaced campsites just off the sandy beach. In fact, this campground occupies the same general region of Rock Island as the early Indian villages and La Salle's trading post.

For the most privacy, five secluded backpacking sites are scattered farther down the Thordarson Loop Trail, with wonderful lake views from atop low bluffs. From our isolated site, sheltered in the carpetlike softness of a cedar grove, we watched loons cruising on the lake. Other frequent companions were cedar waxwings, who cheered us with their gentle chirps, a whistle with a twist.

Rock Island is big enough to provide a variety of scenery along several different trails, and small enough that day hikers can travel all the way around the island (six and a half miles). Day visitors and campers alike may find surprises along the way—deer watching silently from the forest, or the time-worn face of an Indian peering motionless from a cliff wall (one of several rock carvings sculpted by a craftsman during Thordarson's residency).

STONINGTON AND GARDEN PENINSULAS

Reaching southward from Lake Michigan's northern shores are the Stonington and Garden peninsulas. These off-the-beaten-path points of land have not seen the degree of tourism and commercial development of more southerly peninsulas, and retain much of their wilder natures. The farther onto the peninsula you venture, the more solitude you find. Here nature remains unmanicured, less fenced in.

Much of the Stonington Peninsula is Hiawatha National Forest land. A drive south along County Road 513 is well worth the time, with frequent views

Toft Point and Baileys Harbor Bay, on the east shore of the Door Peninsula.

of Little Bay De Noc. As the road nears the peninsula's tip, the last mile narrows into a wonderfully winding drive among the twisted and gnarled trunks of a cedar grove. At the tip are Peninsula Point Light (open to the public), picnic grounds, and a nearly timeless view of open Green Bay.

Significant portions of the Garden Peninsula are state-owned, including Fayette State Park and Lake Superior State Forest land. On the peninsula's western shores are dramatic limestone cliffs of the Niagaran Escarpment. One of these cliffs is a prominent feature at Fayette, where remains of the 19th century iron-smelting town are preserved. On the eastern shore of the Garden Peninsula, the remote and peaceful Portage Bay State Forest Campground is tucked in a scenic cove. Rustic two-track roads lead through sections of state forest land; these become increasingly rugged heading toward the peninsula's southern tip, Point Detour. This area, described as "one of the most remote areas of the state," offers wild beauty and solitude — and also a good chance of getting your vehicle mired in the deep mud or sand of unmaintained trails.

LAKE MICHIGAN SCENIC HIGHWAY: U.S. HIGHWAY 2

Bordering Lake Michigan's north shore between

Naubinway and St. Ignace is a long stretch of U.S. Highway 2, with an abundance of scenic views, roadside parks, and turnouts. The road follows the lakeshore closely, through alternating sections of wild dune and wetland. Distant lighthouses and islands dot the horizon. Punctuating the shoreline are rocky shoals and islets — and numerous small streams that meander around until they enter the lake almost as an afterthought. The Cut River Bridge provides an expansive view of the deep river valley below and the freshwater sea beyond.

Much of the land along U.S. Highway 2 belongs to Lake Superior State Forest and Hiawatha National Forest; each provides a scenic campground on the lake. Here also are some of the finest swimming beaches found anywhere, with beauty and accessibility that lure many passers-by to spontaneously stop and play. Frolicking in the surf is a delightful mix of people of all ages and backgrounds. As diverse as the lake is, so is the diversity of the people attracted to it.

STRAITS OF MACKINAC

The Straits of Mackinac are the meeting place of the upper lakes. Here Lake Michigan joins Lake Huron; and just to the east, Lake Superior's waters empty into Lake Huron. This area has been an important wa-

Autumn view from Skyline Road, Peninsula State Park.

ter crossroads throughout history—vessels ranging from birchbark canoes to modern "long ships" have passed through the three-hundred-foot-deep strait. In 1957, it became a highway crossroads, when the Mackinac Bridge—spanning five miles across the Straits of Mackinac—gracefully linked Michigan's upper and lower peninsulas. Motorists driving as high as two hundred feet above the water enjoy spectacular views of an expanse of water that dwarfs nearby human activities.

In contrast to bustling Mackinac Island on the Lake Huron side of the bridge, St. Helena Island sits peacefully on the Lake Michigan side. Now nearly deserted, this little island's only activity is centered around the old lighthouse on the island's southeast tip, currently under restoration by the Great Lakes Lighthouse Keepers Association.

In the Straits of Mackinac—the hub of the Upper Great Lakes—historical and modern times are uniquely interwoven. At the base of the Mackinac Bridge, a remarkable modern engineering accomplishment, stand two remnants of the region's wild past. To the east is Mackinac Point Lighthouse, whose light guided sailors through the Straits from 1892 to 1957, when the bridge's presence rendered it unnecessary. To the west is Fort Michilimackinac; this restored fortified community was once a great fur trade center, the site of many a voyageurs' rendezvous, and a base for both exploration and war parties.

The geologic and geographic features that made the Straits of Mackinac an important crossroads throughout history continue their influence on human activities. In spite of this activity, much of the wild natural beauty of the region survives. And so this Great Lakes crossroads bridges peninsulas, lakes, and time.

WILDERNESS STATE PARK

Heading west along the south shore of the Straits of Mackinac, the drive into Wilderness State Park is bounded alternately by North Woods and Lake Michigan shoreline. As visitors pass homes (on private land within park boundaries) and two modern campgrounds, they may initially wonder if the park was misnamed. But wilderness does exist here—in backcountry areas requiring effort to reach. Wilderness State Park occupies one of the largest remaining undeveloped tracts of land in Michigan's lower peninsula—encompassing 8,000 acres and more than thirty miles of Lake Michigan coastline (including a string of islands reaching westward into Lake Michigan).

This park offers a variety of different experiences to its visitors. Most accessible are the two campgrounds on or near the lakeshore, picnic areas, and scenic drives. To more fully experience the park's wild character requires hiking or mountain-biking over the more than twelve miles of trails. Bicycling along Sturgeon Bay and South Boundary trails in August, we were pleasantly surprised to encounter not one other person in miles of travel.

Trails guide visitors through wetlands, pines and cedars, and onto rocky Waugoshance Point. Rare and endangered wildflowers, including orchids and dwarf lake iris, can be found with careful search (and we do mean *careful*—we have seen calypso orchids trampled by over-eager admirers). A multitude of bird species inhabit the park's wetlands and forests or pass through during migration: warblers and songbirds, hawks, waterfowl, and shorebirds (occasionally including the rare piping plover).

Several rental cabins are available by reservation. All but one of these rustic cabins sit near the lakeshore, tucked in private settings among graceful evergreens. There are no "luxury" accommodations—no electricity, running water, or indoor plumbing. Simple basics are provided: bunks, table and chairs, wood stove, outside hand pump for water, and of course, an outhouse. In winter, occupants ski in to cabins—up to three miles.

What is given up in comfort and convenience is gained in solitude and in closeness to the lake and to each other. In summertime, we relished our immediate access to the shore: watching ever-changing clouds roll in from the open horizon, wandering aimlessly at sunset, and taking midnight strolls under a canopy of stars. Wildflowers and pitcher plants filled nearby wetlands, bordered by gnarled cedars. One winter evening, we sat around the wood stove, sharing family stories and songs—toasty warm while a blizzard howled across the lake outside. The next morning, dawn brought a clear view of pastel windrows and abstract wind-carved snow sculptures.

BEAVER ISLAND ARCHIPELAGO

Like its neighbor in the Straits to the east, Beaver Island's principal industry is tourism; however, Beaver Island is not another Mackinac Island. It has a unique character all its own. Approaching St. James Harbor on the *Beaver Islander* ferry (out of Charlevoix), passengers see a simple and unhurried town, without fudge shops or the frenzied press of tourists. Automobiles, not horse-drawn carriages, travel its network of rustic roads. And yet a sense of peacefulness pervades most aspects of Beaver Island life. This largest island in Lake Michigan is surrounded by more than ten smaller islands, creating an archipelago that contains some of the lake's most untouched, natural areas.

Countless human dramas have unfolded in the Beaver Island group. In the 1800s, immigrants from Ireland were drawn to Beaver Island, which reminded

Newport State Park.

Limestone cliff at Fayette State Park, on the Garden Peninsula.

U.S. Highway 2 closely follows Lake Michigan's scenic shoreline.

The Mackinac Bridge is a prominent visual feature of the Straits of Mackinac. Mackinac Point Lighthouse stands at its base.

them of their former island home. Beaver Island became known as "America's Emerald Isle." For many years, Irish fishing families reaped the bounties of the archipelago, considered some of the finest fishing grounds in Lake Michigan. Even today, Irish traditions remain strong on Beaver Island. Another colorful interlude in the island's history was the brief but famous Mormon domination of Beaver Island. From 1848, self-appointed prophet and king James Strang ruled a religious communal society that grew to more than 2,000 members, before his assassination and their dispersal in 1856.

Long before the Mormon and Irish settlers of the 1800s, Beaver Island had been home to untold generations of Native Americans. Archaeologists have found evidence of ancient Indian habitations in the Beaver Island group. On Garden Island, the forest still shelters a sacred Indian cemetery, which has been called "the largest native burial site in the central United States." This sacred spot is believed to hold over 3,500 graves, extending from the present century back into the mists of prehistory. Weatherworn spirit houses still mark some graves, while others are identified by headstones and wooden crosses. In this hallowed forest, the more ancient burials lie unmarked, or perhaps subtly indicated with clues only apparent to the knowing eye.

Descendants of these native peoples still feel emotional and spiritual ties to this island they call *Miniss Kitigan.*

In a Beaver Island field, a nearly four-hundred-foot-diameter circle of boulders has been discovered, with configurations that appear to align with seasonal equinoxes. This might be an ancient stonehenge, a stone circle used as an agricultural calendar as much as 1,000 years ago. For Native Americans, the circle may also have spiritual significance. Archaeologists, astronomers, Native Americans, and other experts continue to investigate this potentially significant find, but the verdict is not yet in. The stones do not have a dramatic visual impact, and offer no startling discoveries for the incidental observer. The circle could be a conglomeration of glacial erratics with alignments that are only coincidences, but amazing coincidences (certainly worth further study, and protection from disruption). The mystery itself tugs at our curiosity and imagination.

In the town of St. James, the island's rich cultural and maritime histories are featured in two museums operated by the Beaver Island Historical Society. Also in town, supplies, gifts, and accommodations are available from family businesses with a pleasant and unpretentious atmosphere. As in many Great Lakes locations, island residents are currently struggling with how to allow growth and development and still preserve the unique peaceful character of their island.

Outside St. James, large stretches of beach and forest remain untouched. Although sections of fields and open meadows dot the island's interior and summer homes line portions of the shoreline, over 30 percent of the island is state forest land. Beaver Island's gravel roads wind through scenic forests and past shoreline vistas. These lightly traveled trails are ideal for bicycling, especially mountain-biking. Two public campgrounds offer a variety of campsites near Lake Michigan — some with lake views. These campgrounds offer a more natural experience than we expected to find on an island with motorized traffic and two small airports. Quiet solitude prevailed at our campsite and the nearby shore. On two different occasions, we watched a curious red fox wander silently through our campsite.

Backpackers on Beaver Island do not have established routes to follow. Some choose to follow the shoreline around the island, while others venture into the seclusion of the interior. In either case, primitive camping is allowed on state land, following state forest regulations. Campers should stop at the sheriff substation in St. James to leave a general itinerary in case of emergency, and to obtain current regulations, information on camping, a map showing the location of state property, and free camping permits.

The Lake Michigan shoreline features beaches and dunes, and a host of scenic coves and points. The island's interior, especially the southern half, is filled with mixed hardwood forests, cedar swamps, streams, bogs, marshes, and several inland lakes. It is in this less-traveled area that hikers are more likely to catch glimpses of wildlife, such as deer, fox, raccoon, and beaver. Coyote music may drift across the breeze in early evening, along with the calls of loons.

Some of the wildest places around Lake Michigan exist on the islands surrounding Beaver Island. Several of these — including Hog, Garden, and High islands — are open to the public, and can be reached by charter boat. Primitive camping is allowed on state land; again, be sure to stop at the sheriff substation before embarking. Most of these islands are encircled by ridges of shallow reefs, and access to shore requires rowing, rafting, or wading. Once on shore, be on the lookout for poison ivy, which grows in abundance throughout the archipelago.

High Island offers the most varied terrain, including sand dunes on its western shore, and a sand spit at its northeast corner. Although only four miles from Beaver Island, High Island is reached by a twelve-mile boat trip from St. James Harbor; trails lead through scenic North Woods, past farm clearings created during settlement by the House of David religious community, and along the tranquil shores of Lake Maria.

SKEGEMOG SWAMP WILDLIFE AREA

Skegemog Swamp . . . the name has a foreboding sound. It brings to mind images straight out of a scary movie: eyes peering from the darkness, shadowy forms lurking and slithering just out of sight. But these are the manifestations of fiction and imagination; in reality, Skegemog has a refreshing and increasingly rare beauty.

Skegemog Swamp Wildlife Area occupies 2,700 acres of undeveloped wetlands bordering the east half of Lake Skegemog (which connects with Lake Michigan's Grand Traverse Bay via Elk Lake and Elk River). The area has been recognized for its outstanding examples of marshes, bogs, fens, and conifer swamps. The wilderness shoreline of Lake Skegemog can be explored by canoe; however, much of the wetlands remains relatively inaccessible to humans — an ideal refuge for such wildlife as black bear, bobcat, otter, mink, weasel, beaver, badger, loons, osprey, and bald eagles.

Fortunately, one portion of the swamp is accessible. Through the efforts of volunteers, a scenic boardwalk meanders through the cedar swamp, providing a way to experience its beauty with dry feet. Sunlight filters through delicate cedar boughs, illuminating their twisted and gnarled trunks. The forest floor is carpeted with luxuriously soft mosses, graceful ferns, and delicate wildflowers. Cedars fill the air with their refreshing aromas. The chirping of little frogs, yodeling of distant loons, and cries of geese overhead all land softly on the ears.

This boardwalk is reached by a one mile-hike that begins at the parking area off Schneider Road and follows a trail along an old railroad grade. Balsam firs bordering this trail announce their presence with their sweet fragrance. At the end of the boardwalk is an observation tower, overlooking a marsh and Skegemog Lake. This is a place in which to spend time, listening to the quietness and experiencing the encircling rhythms of life. An eagle soars overhead; waterfowl splash in the distant open water; a beaver glides silently into tall weeds; a large snapping turtle sinks in and out of sight, searching for food in the shallows.

SLEEPING BEAR DUNES NATIONAL LAKESHORE

Of Lake Michigan's many wilderness remnants, the Sleeping Bear Dunes area is a special treasure — a national treasure, preserved by the establishment of Sleeping Bear Dunes National Lakeshore in 1970. Although its stretches of wilderness are interrupted here and there by private land (including the towns of Empire and Glen Arbor), the park's 70,000 acres give plenty of room in which to find solitude, recreation,

Calypso orchid, Wilderness State Park.

Beyond Hog Island lie Garden Island and Beaver Island, all in the Beaver Island archipelago.

and an amazing scenic diversity. The national lakeshore protects more than sixty miles of shoreline, including the two Manitou Islands. (To give these islands the attention they deserve, they are discussed separately from the Sleeping Bear Dunes mainland.)

Lake Michigan's coastline between Frankfort and Leland holds some of the lake's most dramatic beauty. Perched on high bluffs, great dunes tower as high as 460 feet above the sparkling water. Views from these dunes reveal stunning panoramas of islands and sea, forests and sand. There are also more subtle wild beauties to be discovered, in the quiet forests and shores.

Even a brief visit to Sleeping Bear Dunes National Lakeshore yields an impressive introduction to the area. Stop by the visitor center in Empire, struggle up the 150-foot-high Dune Climb, and follow the scenic route along Pierce Stocking Drive. Aptly described in an interpretive pamphlet as "a road to the top of the dunes," this one-way, single-lane, paved road immerses visitors in over seven miles of nonstop scenic beauty. For bicyclists with good brakes, it provides a challenging but rewarding ride. The drive meanders through a variety of ecosystems, including open dunes, forested dunes (where people often see deer), and three overlooks that reveal spectacular vistas of Lake Michigan, the Manitous, and Sleeping Bear Dunes.

Near the south end of the park, the Platte Plains area features beach dunes, an extensive trail system for hiking and cross-country skiing, and the lower Platte River. This gentle river affords the rare opportunity to canoe through largely undeveloped land to the river-mouth at Lake Michigan. However, it is a popular attraction; for greater solitude, choose a time to paddle when no one else would want to. We arrived on a cold autumn morning, with snowflakes flying in the wind. Bundled appropriately, we did not mind the temperature, and colorful fall foliage cheered the gray sky. While onlookers at the canoe livery pondered our sanity, we set off on our two-hour adventure. Traveling downstream required little effort. We enjoyed watching abundant waterfowl, huge spawning salmon in their persistent upstream journey, and the ever-changing vegetative complexion of the riverbanks— all as we traveled through wetlands, forest, and dune ecosystems on our journey to the freshwater sea.

Sleeping Bear Dunes National Lakeshore offers the most to those who spend time getting to know the area—exploring, listening, and accepting its gifts. On the mainland portion of the national lakeshore, areas of natural beauty lie along the rustic forest roads open to car travel. There are four campgrounds, two of which

Garter snake, Skegemog Swamp.

Skegemog Swamp.

are backcountry campgrounds reached only by foot. Throughout the park, an abundance of hiking trails traverse forests, meadows, and dunes. On open dunes, sand reflects the sun's heat and brightness—hats, sunglasses, suntan lotion, a supply of water, and shoes are highly recommended. (Yes, shoes. Hikers are tempted to go barefoot in the sand, only to return with burned feet.) Hiking on an open dune is a paradoxical experience; you find yourself in a dry, desertlike landscape, with a vast expanse of water reaching to the horizon.

Whether experienced through hiking, canoeing, or driving, Sleeping Bear Dunes National Lakeshore is a place of variety and beauty, both subtle and dramatic. Return trips always produce new and different journeys of discovery. And always on the horizon is the inland sea, with massive dune headlands standing as mute testimony to the creative powers of ice, wind, and water.

SOUTH MANITOU ISLAND

It is remarkable that city dwellers from Lake Michigan's southern shores, in less than a day's drive and in one-and-one-half-hour's ferry crossing, can find themselves on an isolated island. In summertime, daily ferry trips carry passengers from Leland to South Manitou Island, for both short excursions and longer camping adventures. Crossing the Manitou Passage itself is a unique experience, with the Manitou islands and towering mainland dunes visible across the water. The ferry passes North Manitou Shoal Lighthouse, as huge freighters rumble along the international shipping lanes.

South Manitou Island is the site of many first ventures into the wilderness. It is reassuring to know that friendly and capable park rangers headquartered at the former lifesaving station are available to give advice and assistance. Three primitive campgrounds offer seclusion and lake access—and at least a few amenities, such as potable water, outhouses, and community fire rings. Two of these campgrounds are reached by hikes of approximately one and a quarter miles. (Popple Campground is three and a half miles from the boat dock.)

Hiking a little over one mile sounds easy enough, but it can be tortuous to the unprepared and inexperienced. We encountered many exhausted campers trying to hand-carry jugs of water, heavy canvas tents, and large coolers. We fully expected these poor souls to be turned off to island camping after their ordeal. But the gifts of South Manitou worked their magic even on the weary and discouraged. After a few days on the peaceful island, several campers described how they had learned from their mistakes, reorganized, and adjusted their methods. Eyes beamed as they talked of

renewal and rejuvenation from starry nights, quiet strolls along the beach, and soothing rhythms of the surf.

Together, the eight-square-mile island's fragility and popularity make low-impact camping a must. While there are no bears on the island, rangers recommend hanging food bags from trees to keep them out of reach of "micro-bears," chipmunks who will go through packs and even tents to get to food. It seems as if the two most abundant species on South Manitou Island are poison ivy and chipmunks. While poison ivy can be avoided, we encountered reckless chipmunks who dashed across trails, practically under our feet. One hasty fellow actually bonked his hard little head on one of our hiking boots!

With time on an island, daily tensions begin to fade, and we see small wonders that normally escape notice. Each evening as we gazed out at Sleeping Bear Dunes, seven miles across the water, little spiders began their nightly activities at the bluff edge. Top-roping down from overhanging branches, each busily spun its web, until territories overlapped. Then the spider wars began, with "hand-to-hand" combat. The winner was clever; it simply nipped the webs of its foes, sending the losers swinging from the tattered filaments.

Night is a special time in wild places. On a July evening, John wrote in his diary:

After a satisfyingly full day of island exploration, I set out on a nighttime hike, with a warm wind drifting off the lake. A mile passed rapidly and pleasantly, without need of extra light under the full moon. Heading back to camp, the rhythmic trilogy of breath, heartbeat, and footfall was quietly interrupted by a shuffling sound. There in the middle of the path, in the full moonlight, were three toads. Not just any toads, they were TOADS, they were BIG TOADS—BIG OBSTINATE TOADS. When I shined the flashlight on them, they all turned toward me. One big fellow took a single definite hop in my direction and glared at me. These were very assertive toads. Feeling somewhat outnumbered, I carefully stepped over them and continued down the trail. I suppose they were headed somewhere on very important business.

Farther down the trail, I stopped to listen to the gentle night sounds, and was distracted by a faint scratching sound near my feet. It was a mushroom moving slowly and rhythmically back and forth against dried leaves. Now what in the world would possess a mushroom to do such a thing? Kneeling down for a closer look, I discovered a snail dining on this mushroom in the moonlight—seemingly oblivious to my presence. With each pass of its tonguelike radula, the snail's weight moved the mushroom back and forth. This tiny creature had already devoured a portion of the mushroom larger than itself.

In this evening of discovery and contemplation, there were no great insights or major revelations—just the genuinely

Autumn sand cherry on the foredunes at Sleeping Bear Dunes National Lakeshore.

pleasant satisfaction of sharing time with these very different and yet kindred beings.

On South Manitou such intimate encounters are intermixed with experiences of larger dimensions. In the Valley of the Giants, we are dwarfed by towering white cedars, over five hundred years old. Atop the nearby perched dunes, we are surrounded by the expansiveness of dunes, forest, and inland sea. On a bluff overlooking the broken hulk of the *Francisco Morazon* in the water just offshore, our thoughts turn to times of fierce storms and turbulent seas.

South Manitou Island Lighthouse stands as a graceful reminder of the island's significant maritime history. From 1871 to 1958, this lighthouse beacon marked the southern entrance to the Manitou Passage, and signaled the location of the island's excellent harbor—the only natural harbor in the 220-mile voyage from Chicago. Nineteenth century steamers sought this harbor's shelter in storms and the island's timber to fuel their boilers. Today, ranger-guided tours of the lighthouse give the uncommon opportunity to enter a one-hundred-foot tall lighthouse tower and climb its winding stairs to enjoy the panorama from the top.

While South Manitou Island Lighthouse stands as a tribute to the island's past, island life goes on, and little sagas continue to unfold—the daily adventures of wide-eyed campers, spiders in their evening combats, Big Obstinate Toads, and a little snail munching a mushroom in the moonlight.

NORTH MANITOU ISLAND

Of Lake Michigan's wilderness areas, North Manitou Island offers one of the most pristine wilderness experiences. This remote island's 15,000 acres and twenty miles of shoreline allow endless opportunities for exploration and solitude. Except for twenty-seven acres around the former North Manitou Village, the island has been managed as wilderness by the National Park Service since its incorporation into the national lakeshore in 1984. Travel is only by foot (rangers included), cooking is by backpacking stove, water must be filtered or boiled, and camping is allowed anywhere (within certain guidelines). It is entirely possible to set up camp and spend several days without hearing or seeing anyone else. Only occasional distant boat motors and airplane engines break the otherwise uninterrupted flow of natural sounds; civilization seems far away, and time loses its sense of urgency.

During summer months, a ferry from Leland provides transportation to North Manitou Island three times a week. (Charter boats are also available from the mainland.) Once on board the North Manitou ferry during our most recent trip, we learned that the ferry would not land at the village dock (near the ranger station and Village Campground), because of a shifting sandbar blocking dock access. Instead, we would disembark on the south end of the island, along a beach sheltered by Dimmick's Point. And so campers began replanning their itineraries.

On arrival, the ferry nosed up to shore, working back and forth to get as close to the beach as possible. Soon the crew called out: "Take off your shoes and socks, and roll up your pants—it's going to be a wet landing!" A ramp at the bow was lowered into the shallow water, giving a rather steep descent. On this ramp, campers, rangers, and boat crew worked together in bucket brigade fashion to unload all the gear. Barefoot, we all walked the plank to a wet welcome to North Manitou Island.

In spite of any inconvenience, this unanticipated landing had an element of adventure in it, for the lake had dealt us one of her surprises, and it was up to us to adjust. After all, one of the prime characteristics of a wilderness experience is the challenge of dealing with the unexpected. Standing on the uninhabited shore as the departing ferry shrank on the horizon, it all seemed appropriate. We had come looking for wilderness, and this certainly felt like it.

The little group of backpackers soon dispersed. Some headed into the forest, others along the beach. One couple, who had apparently counted on camping at the Village Campground near the boat dock, simply stepped off three hundred feet from the Lake Michigan high-water mark (according to regulations), and set up camp. There was a sense of freedom—no hurry to reach a designated campsite within certain time constraints. We could all go where our curiosity led us, and stop when we were ready. As North Manitou grows in popularity, this freedom to choose a campsite carries with it the strong responsibility to leave the island without traces of our passing—to preserve the wild areas and the quiet atmosphere for the enjoyment of all.

On North Manitou, backpackers tramp along the beach, or through forests and meadows on a system of trails left from the island's days of settlement. There are several inland lakes, dunes and bluffs along the western shore (which become especially steep and eroded to the northwest), and seemingly endless North Woods.

The forests have an unusually open look, the result of over-browsing by a deer population that boomed in the absence of natural predators. Seven deer were introduced to the island in 1927 for hunting purposes and fed through the winters by private owners of the island. These original seven propagated a herd numbering 2,000 by 1981.

While the open forests have an attractive, parklike appearance, it is an unhealthy situation. Vegetation preferred by deer is devastated—strawberries, trilli-

Beneath the stars, the South Manitou Island Lighthouse tower is illuminated by moonglow.

Backpackers unload gear from the North Manitou Island ferry, Manitou Isle.

North Manitou Island shore at sunset.

ums, and saplings of white pines, cedars, and maples. The loss of these young trees leaves none to replace older ones as they die. At the same time, species unpalatable to deer, such as beech, grow unchecked. The eventual result is a forest of decreased diversity and increased susceptibility to disease.

It was also unhealthy for the deer, who suffered large winter die-offs. These die-offs and the introduction of controlled hunting dropped the population to an estimated five hundred by 1989. While people see deer less commonly, these shy creatures still grace the island's forests and shores. Our most frequent encounters were auditory—in the evenings, we often heard deer huffing outside the tent. Were they expressing concern over the unexpected presence of our tent in their familiar woods?

Another island resident previously introduced by humans is not so shy—the raccoon. These clever, initially endearing creatures, having learned that backpackers bring food with them, often become bold nuisances. Food should never be stored inside tents, but rather hung suspended by rope between two trees, at least six feet above ground. Improper techniques can lead to results that, while frustrating to campers, are not without their humor. One ranger described a chaotic scene he encountered, when a group of Boy Scouts hung food bags between trees, but only a couple of feet off the ground. Summoned to help, he found frazzled scouts helplessly watching as furry masked bandits batted the food bags like piñatas. Food flew everywhere, while the eyes of masked reinforcements watched from the perimeter of the campsite.

Chipmunks are as prevalent on North Manitou as they are on South Manitou. However, in contrast to its sister island, North Manitou has very little poison ivy. As with siblings the world over, the two islands have many similarities and differences. The dangers of the Manitou Passage gave each island a lighthouse and lifesaving station. In the days when water transportation dominated the region, both islands were home to settlers, farmers, fishermen, and lumbermen. At one time, two villages existed on North Manitou. Crescent City, a lumber town on the island's west shore, even had a small railroad, six miles long. While few traces of Crescent City remain, a number of buildings in North Manitou Village still stand, empty and weathered.

The view from campsites on the south and west sides of North Manitou is of its sister island floating gracefully on the horizon. Only three miles across the water, South Manitou appears and disappears in the mist, and makes a striking silhouette in the sunset afterglow. From the east side of North Manitou, the mainland is a thin strip on the horizon, with distant freighters and sailboats passing in between. These peaceful vistas are ample reward for carrying a heavy pack over miles of forest trails and sandy beaches. In the wilderness of North Manitou, we enjoyed exhilarating day hikes, as well as the unhurried relaxation of a rainy day, when we swung in protected hammocks and drank in the beauty of cedars, birches, and water.

North Manitou Island is unique in our modern world. While many wildlands are rapidly disappearing into "civilization," here this trend has been reversed. The once-bustling island is being allowed to revert to its wilderness state. North Manitou Island offers to its visitors, in the words of the National Park Service, "a primitive experience emphasizing solitude, a feeling of self-reliance and a sense of exploration."

LOOKING BACK

A chill was in the air, and fall's riot of colors fading, as our travels for this book drew to a close. Our explorations of Lake Michigan's wild areas will never end, but it was time for an interlude—for writing, and for the girls' education. On our final weekend trip, we returned to favorite places at Sleeping Bear Dunes National Lakeshore.

After dark, settled in at our campsite in D.H. Day Campground, we were lured to the beach by the relentless call of the surf. Standing at the water's edge had become a familiar experience, and yet somehow always new. There under the shimmering stars and glow of a full moon, we were once again renewed by the wild beauty all about us. The broad stretch of beach, dune headlands to either side, and silver wave crests were all transformed by moonlight into a scene of luminous dimensions. On the horizon, we recognized our old friends, the Manitou islands, and recalled sitting on their isolated shores, contemplating the distant mainland where we now stood. Touching the water, we were instantly connected to all the wonderful places we had experienced—and to the wild nature of the lake.

This reverie was broken as we shivered in the wintry air. It was time to go. Heading back toward camp, we surprised a deer in the small beach dunes. As it bounded across the trail only yards in front of us, moonlight caught its white flag tail, which flitted phantomlike over the dunes in that bright night.

EPILOGUE

When we try to pick out anything by itself, we find it hitched to everything else in the universe.
— John Muir

Books, like road maps, are symbols that tell you how to find something, but they cannot supply the experience. We encourage you to go and seek your own Lake Michigan adventures, your own journeys of discovery. For us, it has been a pleasant surprise; like the early explorers, we came seeking less than we ultimately found. More wildness endures in this inland sea than most people realize.

We have long known Lake Michigan—specializing as photographers and writers in the Great Lakes and North Woods, and living within three miles of the lake for over twelve years. But previously, we had looked at pieces of the lake, small microcosms of the whole. Never before had we the extended opportunity to develop an intimate relationship with the Lake Michigan Basin as an entity. Islands and peninsulas . . . woodlands and wetlands . . . dunes, ducks, and dwarf lake iris . . . terns, turtles, and people . . . they are all inextricably tied up in one large, and very wild, interdependent knot.

Also bound up in this life and beauty are the equally complicated and interwoven results of years of environmental abuses by our species—abuses of global scope, affecting not only Lake Michigan, but every ecosystem on earth. In the growing awareness of crisis in this planet that is our life source, it appears that the tides of human attitudes are beginning to turn. The human species stands on the brink of past and present destructiveness, and potential future reconciliation. Something is beginning to stir in the human community—awakening ancient perceptions in modern contexts, and rekindling our emotional and spiritual relationship with the larger sacred community of life forms that surrounds us.

Cobblestone beach, Porte des Morts.

INDEX TO WILDERNESS REMNANTS

REFERENCES

Ashworth, William. *The Late, Great Lakes*. New York: Alfred A. Knopf, 1986.

Bacig, Tom, and Fred Thompson. *Tall Timber: A Pictorial History of Logging in the Upper Midwest*. Bloomington, Minn.: Voyageur Press, 1982.

Barnes, Burton V., and Warren H. Wagner, Jr. *Michigan Trees: A Guide to the Trees of Michigan and the Great Lakes Region*. Ann Arbor: University of Michigan Press, 1981.

Beaver Island Historical Society. *The Journal of Beaver Island History*. Vol. 2. St. James, Mich.: Beaver Island Historical Society, 1980.

Beeson, Lewis, ed. *This is Michigan: A Sketch of These Times and Times Gone By*. Lansing: Michigan Historical Commission, 1949.

Benyus, Janine M. *Northwoods Wildlife: A Watcher's Guide to Habitats*. Minocqua, Wisc.: Northword Press, Inc., 1989.

Bogue, Margaret Beattie. *Around the Shores of Lake Michigan: A Guide to Historic Sites*. Madison: University of Wisconsin Press, 1985.

Conrader, Jay M., and Constance Conrader. *Northwoods Wildlife Region*. Happy Camp, Cal.: Naturegraph Publishers, Inc., 1984.

Daniel, Glenda. *Dune Country: A Hiker's Guide to the Indiana Dunes*. Athens, Ohio: Swallow Press, 1984.

Daniel, Glenda, and Jerry Sullivan. *A Sierra Club Naturalist's Guide to the North Woods of Michigan, Wisconsin, Minnesota and Southern Ontario*. San Francisco: Sierra Club Books, 1981.

Devault, David. Telephone conversation with authors. 28 November 1989.

Dochoda, Marg. Telephone conversation with authors. 21 November 1989.

Dorr, John A., and Donald F. Eschman. *Geology of Michigan*. Ann Arbor: University of Michigan Press, 1970.

Eder, Tim, and John Jackson. *A Citizens' Guide to the Great Lakes Water Quality Agreement*. Buffalo, N.Y.: Great Lakes United, 1988.

Ellis, William Donohue. *Land of the Inland Seas: The Historic and Beautiful Great Lakes Country*. Palo Alto, Cal.: American West Publishing Company, 1974.

Emery, Lee. *Review of Fish Species Introduced into the Great Lakes, 1819–1974*. Technical Report No. 45. Ann Arbor, Mich.: Great Lakes Fishery Commission, 1985.

Engel, J. Ronald. *Sacred Sands*. Middletown, Conn.: Wesleyan University Press, 1983.

Environment Canada, United States Environmental Protection Agency, Brock University, and Northwestern University. *The Great Lakes: An Environmental Atlas and Resource Book*. Chicago and Toronto: United States Environmental Protection Agency Great Lakes National Program Office and Environment Canada, Conservation and Protection, Ontario Region, 1987.

Eshenroder, Randy. "A Perspective on Artificial Fishery Systems for the Great Lakes." Paper presented at Wild Trout IV, Yellowstone National Park, 18–19 September 1989.

Farrand, W. R. *The Glacial Lakes around Lake Michigan*. Bulletin 4, Geological Survey Division. Lansing: Michigan Department of Natural Resources, 1987.

Fitting, James E. *The Prehistory of the Burnt Bluff Area*. Anthropological Papers, Museum of Anthropology, University of Michigan, No. 34. Ann Arbor: University of Michigan, 1968.

Francis, George R., John J. Magnuson, Henry A. Regier, and Daniel R. Talhelm, eds. *Rehabilitating Great Lakes Ecosystems*. Technical Report No. 37. Ann Arbor, Mich.: Great Lakes Fishery Commission, 1979.

Frazier, Jean. *Kah-wam-da-meh*. Grand Ledge, Mich.: Herman E. Cameron Memorial Foundation, Inc., 1989.

Great Lakes Natural Resource Center. "Summary of Quantitative Health Assessments for PCBs, DDT, Dieldrin, and Chlordane." National Wildlife Federation. Photocopy.

Great Lakes United. *The Great Lakes United*, Vol. 3, Nos. 3–4; Vol. 4, No. 3. 1988–1989.

Guyton, Arthur C., M.D. *Textbook of Medical Physiology.* 4th ed. Philadelphia: W.B. Saunders Company, 1971.

Harris, H. J. Telephone conversation with authors. 30 November 1989.

Hatt, Robert T., Josselyn Van Tyne, Laurence C. Stuart, Clifford H. Pope, and Arnold B. Grobman. *Island Life: A Study of the Land Vertebrates of the Islands of Eastern Lake Michigan.* Cranbrook Institute of Science Bulletin No. 27. Bloomfield Hills, Mich.: Cranbrook Press, 1948.

Herdendorf, Charles E., C. Nicholas Raphael, and Eugene Jaworski. *The Ecology of Lake St. Clair Wetlands: A Community Profile.* Biological Report 85(7.7). Washington, D.C.: National Wetlands Research Center, Fish and Wildlife Service, September 1986.

Hirthe, Walter M., and Mary K. Hirthe. *Schooner Days in Door County.* Minneapolis, Minn.: Voyageur Press, 1986.

Hough, Jack L. *Geology of the Great Lakes.* Urbana: University of Illinois Press, 1958.

Humphrey, Harold. Telephone conversation with authors. 22 November 1989.

Hyde, Charles K. *The Northern Lights: Lighthouses of the Upper Great Lakes.* Lansing, Mich.: Two Peninsula Press, 1986.

Kitchell, Jim. Telephone conversation with authors. 21 November 1989.

Kogan, Herman, and Robert Cromie. *The Great Fire: Chicago 1871.* New York: G.P. Putnam's Sons, 1971.

Kubiak, T. J., and H. J. Harris, L. M. Smith, T. R. Schwartz, D. L. Stalling, J. A. Trick, L. Sileo, D. E. Docherty, and T. C. Erdman. "Microcontaminants and Reproductive Impairment of the Forster's Tern on Green Bay, Lake Michigan — 1983." *Archives of Environmental Contamination and Toxicology* 18 (1989): 706–27.

Kuchenberg, Tom. *Reflections in a Tarnished Mirror: The Use and Abuse of the Great Lakes.* Sturgeon Bay, Wisc.: Golden Glow Publishing, 1978.

Lake Michigan Federation. *Lake Michigan: The Bulletin of the Lake Michigan Federation.* Fall 1984, Spring 1985, Summer 1985, Fall 1985, Spring 1986, Summer 1986, Fall 1987.

Ludwig, Jim. Telephone conversation with authors. 27 November 1989.

Lukes, Roy. *The Ridges Sanctuary: Its History, Geology, Plants, and Animals.* Baileys Harbor, Wisc.: Ridges Sanctuary, 1988.

Lyons, Janet, and Sandra Jordan. *Walking the Wetlands.* New York: John Wiley & Sons, Inc., 1989.

Maher, Mary. *The Places We Save.* Madison: Wisconsin Chapter of the Nature Conservancy, 1988.

Mason, Ronald J. *Rock Island: Historical Indian Archaeology in the Northern Lake Michigan Basin.* MCJA Special Paper No. 6. Kent, Ohio: Kent State University Press, 1986.

McMurray, John, and Mal Sillars. *Weather for Great Lakes Sailors.* Flint, Mich.: Commercial Weather Services, Inc., 1980.

Michigan Sea Grant College Program. *Shoreline Erosion — Questions and Answers.* rev. ed. Ann Arbor: Michigan Sea Grant College Program Publications Office, 1985.

Mortimer, Clifford H. *Environmental Status of the Lake Michigan Region.* Vol. 2, *Physical Limnology of Lake Michigan.* ANL/ES-1, Argonne National Laboratory.

National Ocean Survey. *United States Coast Pilot 6.* Washington, D.C.: National Ocean Survey, 1982.

National Oceanic and Atmospheric Administration. *Great Lakes Water Levels, 1860–1989.* Washington, D.C.: National Oceanic and Atmospheric Administration, 1989.

National Wildlife Federation. *Lake Michigan Sport Fish: Should You Eat Your Catch?.* Washington, D.C.: National Wildlife Federation, 1989.

Olson, Sigurd F. *Open Horizons.* New York: Alfred A. Knopf, 1985.

Palmquist, John C., ed. *Wisconsin's Door Peninsula: A Natural History.* Appleton, Wisc.: Perin Press, 1989.

Platt, Rutherford. *The Great American Forest.* Englewood Cliffs, N.J.: Prentice-Hall, Inc., 1965.

Powers, Tom. *Natural Michigan.* Davison, Mich.: Friede Publications, 1987.

Project Management Team, International Joint Commission. "Living with the Lakes: Challenges and Opportunities." Progress Report to the International Joint Commission, July 1989. Photocopy.

Quaife, Milo M. *Lake Michigan.* Indianapolis: Bobbs-Merrill Company, 1944.

Quimby, George, I. *Indian Life in the Upper Great Lakes.* Chicago: University of Chicago Press, 1960.

Ratigan, William. *Great Lakes Shipwrecks and Survivals.* Grand Rapids, Mich.: Wm. B. Eerdmans Publishing Company, 1977.

Ritzenthaler, Robert E. *Prehistoric Indians of Wisconsin.* 3d ed., revised by Lynne G. Goldstein. Milwaukee, Wisc.: Milwaukee Public Museum, 1985.

Scharf, William C. Telephone conversation with authors. 5 May 1990.

Seno, William Joseph, ed. *Up Country: Voices from the Midwestern Wilderness.* Madison, Wisc.: Round River Publishing Company, 1985.

Sloane, Eric. *Eric Sloane's Weather Book.* New York: Hawthorn Books, Inc., 1949.

Sommers, Lawrence M. "Lake Michigan, Underwater." *Michigan Natural Resources Magazine,* July/August 1983.

Tanner, Helen Hornbeck, ed. *Atlas of Great Lakes Indian History.* Norman and London: University of Oklahoma Press.

Thibodeau, Francis R. "An Economic Analysis of Wetland Protection." *Journal of Environmental Management* 12 (1981): 19–30.

University of Wisconsin Sea Grant Institute. "Eating Lake Michigan Fish." Madison: University of Wisconsin Sea Grant Institute, June 1989.

Van Matre, Steve, and Bill Weiler, eds. *The Earth Speaks.* Warrenville, Ill.: Institute for Earth Education, 1983.

Vent, Myron H. *South Manitou Island: From Pioneer Community to National Park.* 1973. Reprint. New York: Eastern National Park & Monument Association, 1980.

Walker, Louise Jean. *Legends of Green Sky Hill.* Grand Rapids, Mich.: Wm. B. Eerdmans Publishing Company, 1959.

Wallace, David Rains. *Life in the Balance.* San Diego: Harcourt Brace Jovanovich, 1987.

Weeks, George. *Sleeping Bear: Its Lore, Legends and First People.* Glen Arbor: Cottage Book Shop of Glen Arbor and Historical Society of Michigan, 1988.

Weiner, Jonathan. *Planet Earth.* New York: Bantam Books, 1986.

Well, LaRue, and Alberton L. McLain. *Lake Michigan: Man's Effects on Native Fish Stocks and Other Biota.* Technical Report No. 20. Ann Arbor, Mich.: Great Lakes Fishery Commission, 1973.

Wells, Robert W., and Don Davenport. *Fire and Ice.* Ashland, Wisc.: Northword, Inc., 1983.